COOL
careers

for
girls

in

Travel &
Hospitality

Also in the same series

Cool Careers for Girls in Air & Space

Cool Careers for Girls with Animals

Cool Careers for Girls in Computers

Cool Careers for Girls as Crime Solvers

Cool Careers for Girls in Construction

Cool Careers for Girls in Engineering

Cool Careers for Girls as Environmentalists

Cool Careers for Girls in Food

Cool Careers for Girls in Health

Cool Careers for Girls in Law

Cool Careers for Girls in Performing Arts

Cool Careers for Girls in Sports

IMPACT PUBLICATIONS

COOL careers

for
girls

in

Travel &
Hospitality

CEEL PASTERNAK

Library of Congress Cataloging-in-Publication Data

Pasternak, Ceel, 1932-
   Cool careers for girls in travel and hospitality / Ceel Pasternak.
     p. cm.--(Cool careers for girls; 13)
   Includes bibliographical references and index.
   ISBN 1-57023-192-3 paper
   ISBN 1-57023-193-1 hardcover

                              2002109076

Publisher: For information on Impact Publications, including current and forthcoming publications, authors, press kits, bookstore, and submission requirements, visit Impact's Web site: www.impactpublications.com

Publicity/Rights: For information on publicity, author interviews, and subsidiary rights, contact the Public Relations and Marketing Department: Tel. 703/361-7300 or Fax 703/335-9486.

Sales/Distribution: All paperback bookstore sales are handled through Impact's trade distributor: National Book Network, 15200 NBN Way, Blue Ridge Summit, PA 17214, Tel. 1-800-462-6420. All other sales and distribution inquiries should be directed to the publisher: Sales Department, IMPACT PUBLICATIONS, 9104-N Manassas Dr., Manassas Park, VA 20111-5211, Tel. 703/361-7300, Fax 703/335-9486, or E-mail: coolcareers@impactpublications.com

Book design by Guenet Abraham
Desktopped by C. M. Grafik

Dedicated to the women who were
kind enough to share their stories
in this book

Contents

HOSPITALITY CAREERS

A Special Introduction by Karen Ulrich

Faculty, Hospitality Department, Paul Smith's College, Paul Smiths, NY

Do you like to travel and meet new people who may be very different from yourself? Do you like to use the computer? Do you like helping people get organized? Are you a good writer or speaker? A career in the travel or hospitality industry may be a good choice for you.

Thanks to computers and a mobile global market, the world of travel is changing quickly. Travel agencies are becoming more specialized and service-oriented to attract customers, since most people can make vacation plans online.

Adventure tourism is becoming more popular. What is adventure tourism?, you might ask. It's taking a vacation to somewhere that has exciting outdoor activities such as whitewater rafting, mountain climbing, para-skiing, and hiking through exotic locations. For these adventures, people will need a travel agent familiar with adventure travels and a tour guide—someone who can show them how to do the adventure (like mountain climbing) and keep them from getting lost or hurt. If you're not the adventure type, there are several other options and directions possible in the travel field including, but certainly not limited to, the professions you will read about in this book.

The hospitality field is changing as quickly as the travel business, offering new directions you can take your career to. People used to think that working in the hospitality field meant working at the front desk of a hotel and smiling at the guest. While the front desk at a hotel is important, women are successful in all aspects of the hospitality industry, including top management. Some of the women you will read about in this book may have planned much of their young lives to go into the field they are in now, and some may have just fallen into it and found they just happened to love it.

Let's think for a second about what hospitality really means. It means making someone feel comfortable and at home while they are away from home. It means looking out for the needs of your guests. It means making the guests feel like their money is well spent because you are looking after their every need and want, and you can give them things they didn't even know they needed or wanted. Hospitality means making all this happen in such a way that it looks effortless and graceful and it's done with a smile, even on days when one may not quite feel like smiling. As you will read in this book, the hospitality business can be hard work, but it can be fun at the same time. You will meet people from lots of different places, who may not speak the same language as you, nor dress the same as you, nor even eat the same food as you. Learning more about them and where they're from makes the job interesting and challenging.

If this job is such hard work, why did I go into it? Well, I was on vacation with my parents when I was 13. We accidentally ended up at a beautiful hotel with a restaurant. It happened to be later in the evening, and we decided to eat at the hotel's restaurant. When our food came, it wasn't just on plates that were put down in front of us. A waiter and a cart accompanied our food. On the cart was a portable burner. He prepared our food at the tableside and served it right there in the dining room. I decided right there that I wanted to be able to impress people by doing something like that. I guess I wanted to be a show-off! Eventually, I got into the hospitality business and loved doing it. Now, I teach classes in how to work in the hospitality field.

What are some future possibilities in the hospitality and travel businesses? People are going to continue to travel and will need places to stay. They want to see the famous attractions and local sites and visit eateries. People like to have options for things to do on vacations. Not too far in the future, space and space stations will become a popular destination for people who can afford the trip. When you think about that possibility, there are lots of new directions for jobs in hospitality and travel. Someone will need to make

arrangements for the travel to be possible, guests will need a place to stay, guests will need to be fed, and above all guests will need to be comfortable, or they won't do it again or recommend it to their friends.

If you're interested in travel and hospitality, reading this book is a start on your "journey." Each story will provide you with an understanding of a typical day on the job, educational requirements, challenges and rewards, salaries, and employment opportunities. You will also find a checklist with clues about what personality types and lifestyles are most suitable to a particular job. In the final chapter, the women profiled offer advice on what you can do now. You'll find recommendations on books to read and where to find further information.

I suggest that you take classes in foreign languages, speaking and writing skills, cultural diversity, psychology, and interpersonal communications. Also, consider getting an after-school job or a summer job in the some part of the field, even if it's scooping ice cream or housekeeping in a hotel.

Remember that the jobs will vary in fun and excitement, but most days you'll love going to work.

COOL
careers

for
girls

in

Travel &
Hospitality

CEEL PASTERNAK

Amanda Reid

Amanda Reid

Social Hostess, aboard *Constellation*, Celebrity Cruises, Miami, FL

Cruise Ship
Social Hostess

A Warm Welcome Aboard

As people arrive at the Celebrity Cruises ship, *Constellation*, Amanda Reid is one of the first people they meet. She is there as social hostess to welcome them aboard.

"I feel that embarkation day is such an important day as we make that first impression. I try to meet as many passengers as possible as they check in. I really try to make guests feel welcome, and I enjoy recognizing the many guests who have cruised with us before."

Amanda is easily recognized because she wears a uniform with a name badge. She has a day uniform and an evening uniform. "On formal dress nights I wear my own clothes—conservative evening wear is my choice and personal style." Her days usually start between 8:30 and 9 a.m. and end around 11 p.m., but she often

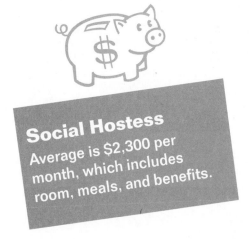

Social Hostess
Average is $2,300 per month, which includes room, meals, and benefits.

Wants to be
ballet dancer, starts
lessons at age four

Continues ballet and
takes up tennis as a teen

Trains at classical
ballet school in
London

gets a break in the afternoons for a couple hours. "Embarkation day is the longest and most tedious for me. On average, I work around 14 hours, all of it on my feet!"

The ship is really a large, floating, luxurious hotel, with several dining ter to an appropriate department head, working to change a negative to a positive experience. "I like to spend most evenings in the main dining room, going from table to table greeting and chatting. This is the best way to get feedback from the guests. I ask

I spend most evenings in the main dining room, going from table to table greeting and chatting. This is the best way to get feedback from the guests.

areas, swimming pools, gift shops, entertainment areas, and fitness facilities. Amanda's job is best described as looking after the needs of the guests— answering questions, listening attentively and thoughtfully to a guest's problem, sometimes taking the mat- them how their day was, and if there are any questions or problems. They may have a question about an upcoming shore visit. If I don't have the answer, I make a quick call to find out."

"One night, I was in the ship's main restaurant and spoke with a lady who

had fallen while ashore. She had her leg in a cast and was in a wheelchair. She mentioned to me that she was finding it very difficult to manage simple things like getting into the bathroom. So, I spoke with our guest relations manager to explain the problem to him. Fortunately, he had a handicapped cabin available. This allowed me to return to the dining room to tell the guest this pleasant news, and she was so grateful."

While socializing takes up the greater portion of Amanda's working hours, she has other responsibilities. She coordinates the invitations for dinners at the Captain's table and for dinners with the other senior officers as well. These normally take place on formal nights. She also assists in hosting the "Captain's Club" (repeat guests' club) cocktail party. "We also hold a special party for couples celebrating their honeymoon or anniversary during each cruise, and I am responsible for arranging this as well. On the days at sea, I like to add some activities, like a class in scarf-tying or napkin folding. I also introduce the wine tasting events and culinary demonstrations on board."

"On a more somber note, I also am sometimes called by the medical department to assist if they have an emergency of any kind, perhaps to comfort the spouse."

Ports of Call

Amanda has a contract with Celebrity Cruises which details her duties, her pay, and her benefits for a period of time. "On this contract, I am working on Celebrity Cruises'

7

AMANDA'S CAREER PATH

Joins Celebrity
Cruises, teaches
choreography
and dances

Becomes social
hostess

newest ship, *Constellation*, cruising in the Mediterranean, Norwegian Fjords, around the United Kingdom and the Baltic throughout the summer. All the itineraries are fantastic and interesting. I have been to most of the ports before, so I already know where the good shopping and eateries are."

The travel, of course, is a major plus in working on cruise ships. "We cruise to some wonderful areas—Alaska, the Greek Islands, South America, Hawaii, the Panama Canal, and more. Because I have a very fair complexion, I do not relish baking in the sun and, as a rule, tend to stay out of it. So naturally, the Caribbean itineraries do not hold as great an appeal for me personally. But having said that, most of the ships change their itineraries during the winter months

and descend on the many lush islands in the Caribbean Sea, so I do get to spend copious time in the hot weather if I choose to."

A Second Home

After so many years at sea, Amanda considers the ship her second home. (She grew up in the town of Folkestone on the southeast coast of England and still lives there today.)

"I am fortunate to have a cabin to myself and I treasure this, as most of the crew share accommodations. Our cabins onboard are well-equipped with TVs, VCRs, and small refrigerators. Every cabin also has its own small bathroom with shower, and a cabin steward cleans the cabin every day and changes the towels and so forth. It is wonderful to be around the guests and chat with them, but I am the type of person who also needs to have some 'down time.' So, after an evening of constant conversation, I like to get back to my cabin and just 'veg' in front of the TV for awhile before bedtime. Occasionally I will go for a drink with 'the girls,' maybe venture into the staff bar, or watch one of the shows, but I finish most of my evenings quietly watching TV in my cabin. I also like to read, so I always have a good novel to enjoy."

"My closest friends on board the ship include the program coordinator, European hostess, and future sales consultant. We are a small group who have worked together for some years now. Our daily schedules are all different, but we normally try to get together for lunch in the officers' mess and often manage to get ashore in one of the ports for shopping and exploring local restaurants. There are different eating areas for the crew, staff, and officers, and I have to say that the food provided is excellent."

CAREER CHECKLIST ✓

You'll like this job if you …

- Care about people's well being
- Enjoy solving problems
- Will work hard as member of a team
- Enjoy meeting new people
- Are comfortable with cultures different from yours
- Like to travel

A Dancer at Heart

Amanda's first job on a cruise ship was as a dancer. Being a dancer was her childhood dream and her career. She started classical ballet classes at the age of four. "When I was not actually in the dance studio with the other children, I spent many hours dressed in my tutu posing in front of Mum's full length mirror. I never wanted to be anything else but a classical dancer."

During the teen years, "I went through a period of anxiety as I saw 'puppy fat' pounds increase my weight, and my physique changed. I began to think that this might be the end of my career as a dancer. I still attended many classes; however, I also became very keen on tennis and swung my enthusiasm to the courts. I was good enough to get onto the school tennis team."

Both Amanda's parents were athletic and good tennis players. Her father was also quite musical and played piano. "I grew up listening to classical music, learning to love it. I was also a Beatles fan and loved the music of the 60s and 70s—from the Doors and Motown to the Beach Boys and Elvis. The first two records I purchased were 'I Heard It Through the Grapevine' and the ballet music, 'Swan Lake'."

She decided for her it must be classical ballet or nothing. "So it was nothing for almost a year while I attended classes and auditions." She joined a small ballet group, but after one performance of "Sylphide," where she was

I try to get together with my three best friends for lunch in the officers' mess and often manage to get ashore in one of the ports for shopping and exploring local restaurants.

In her later teens, Amanda slimmed down, and at age 16 went to a classical ballet school in London where she trained for three years. Her first professional job was in a Christmas pantomime in London. Then she took a job in Spain as principal dancer in a cabaret (a restaurant serving liquor and providing entertainment), where she had a classical solo.

Her next job was in a cabaret, but she did not perform classical dancing.

a Sylph, the company closed. Next, she passed an audition for a ballet company in Perth, Australia, and thought her career had finally turned. Unfortunately, the contract fell through.

"By then I just had to work. The dance captain on the cruise ship *Queen Elizabeth II (QE2)* saw me in a class in London and told me there was a vacancy I could fill if I could get my visa and be ready in one week. This I did and joined *QE2* in September 1977."

We cruise to some wonderful areas—Alaska, the Greek Islands, South America, Hawaii, the Panama Canal, and more.

Amanda figured she would stay for just the six-month contract. However, after the six months, the dance captain left and Amanda was asked to take his job. "After the next six months, they hired new choreographers to put on new shows and new opening routines, so I stayed. There was always a new challenge to keep me staying. I was with Cunard Line for 12 years."

Dancers were expected to do a great deal of cruise staff work. "I helped out with events going on around the ship and I loved it. I volunteered myself for all sorts of extra work and have a program for 1978 that has me listed as social directress."

In 1989, when she was principal dancer with the entertainer and choreographer Peter Gordeno, he was asked to join the new Celebrity Cruises line. Amanda left Cunard and became his assistant. "I taught his choreography to the dancers and continued to dance until 1992. The hardest decision I ever had to make was to give up my life as a dancer. However, I finally decided after many a morning waking up to the aches and pains of simply getting older, that it was time. I asked to be appointed to the role of social hostess on the new ship *Zenith*."

In Great Company

"Many of the people working on *Constellation* are people I have worked with over the years on other Celebrity ships, which helps create the great atmosphere. We have a huge melting pot of nationalities of crew, staff, and officers. Since the turnover of crew is low, I do get to know them. I consider myself extremely lucky to have a job that I can wake up to in the mornings and look forward to (although embarkation days may be considered an exception to this rule!). I intend to stay with this job for as long as I continue to enjoy it."

"I am often asked if I miss the dancing. The answer is yes, as I am still a dancer at heart. But my life now is as fun and rewarding as it was then; just in a different way. Sometimes, when I don't feel '100%,' and I still have to move around the ship with a smile on my face, I relate to my self-discipline as a dancer, and how one just has to get out on stage no matter what. 'The show must go on.' And I just love my job. I wouldn't trade it for the world."

GROUNDBREAKERS
Journals of Women Travelers

Celia Fiennes wrote about her experiences as she traveled through every county in 17th-century England. A young, single woman, she rode side-saddle accompanied by two servants. In her journal *The Journeys of Celia Fiennes 1685-c.1712*, she wrote about great houses, their furnishings and gardens. She described the famous health "spaws," modern innovations such as the water closet Queen Mary had installed, and details about mines and quarries she visited. She was often critical of the people she met along the way.

Twice she was thrown from her horse when it fell, but suffered "noe harm I bless God."

In America, **Sarah Kemble Knight** (1666-1727) wrote of her round trip from Boston to New York in *The Journal of Madam Knight*. A business woman of high social status, she undertook the journey when she received news about settlement of the estate of a relative. It was a rare woman who would undertake such a journey alone. Her personal writings reveal a strong character overcoming her fears, relating her trying and frightening journey with humor.

Sources: "The Journeys of Celia Fiennes" by Jean Ducey for *British Heritage* magazine, February 1998;
www.endicott.edu/production/academic/library/sarahkembleknight.html

Elizabeth A. Domingue

Elizabeth A. Domingue

Wildlife Biologist and Naturalist, Photographer, and Owner,

Outdoor Adventures, Sevierville, TN

Major, Wildlife Science; master's degree in Wildlife/Conservation

Biology, University of Florida, Gainesville, FL

More Than A Walk
Through the Woods

Interpretive Guide, Naturalist, and Wildlife Biologist

Ever since she can remember, Elizabeth (Liz) Domingue has been interested in wildlife. "My first word as a child was *bird*. I was very excited about birds, plants, mammals, everything. I had ideas about what I wanted to do in my life, and some of the things I do now with my own business are those ideas I had as a kid. I wanted to be involved in learning about plants and wildlife and to teach others about them by writing, drawing, and taking pictures. To be a naturalist has always been my goal."

Liz achieved her goal, and that achievement brought her to her own business, Outdoor Adventures. A big part of Liz's business is to lead interpretive hikes in the Great Smoky Mountains National Park, which lies in North Carolina and Tennessee. (On

Tour Guide

For individual hikes: $50 a day

For environmental education programs: $100 for half day, $200 for full day, $250 for overnight

Total income: People who start their own business may not earn any salary in the beginning. They invest their own money in the business, they get more money through loans or venture capital, and, until they make a profit or "go public" by selling stock, they probably pay themselves a small salary and put profits back into the business to help it grow. Liz's salary averages $30,000 and above.

interpretive hikes, the guide tells the hikers about the plants, wildlife, geology, cultural history, and other aspects of the trail and its surroundings. For example, she will point out birds, salamanders, plants used as medicines, places where Native Americans lived, and how a trail got its name.)

"I lead my own hikes and provide environmental education programs for teachers, school groups, Girl Scouts, families, and for individuals. I lead environmental awareness camps and have photo camps for kids." Liz's education, the research she's done, and her hiking experience have led to many opportunities. Four times a year, she teaches Smoky Mountain Field School's one-day courses in the Park, sponsored by the University of Tennessee. McGraw-Hill (publishers) has asked Liz to write the text for their new Tennessee science textbooks/field guide section, grades 1–5. "They're going to publish some of my photographs, too." Besides leading hikes for her own business, Liz leads hikes for other businesses, including an outdoor sports store and Country Walkers, a company that provides tours for people who want to do interpretive hikes in places all over the world.

Leading the Walkers, Step by Step

Liz already had her own business when a friend told her about Country Walkers. "After I completed a grant-funded research project in Belize (a country in Central America), I switched gears from doing mostly research to education, which mainly

Moves to Florida,
gets master's degree

Researcher in Florida,
photos published

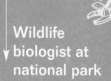
Wildlife
biologist at
national park

consisted of guiding my own interpretive hikes and getting into environmental education." At that time, Country Walkers did not have hiking tours in the Great Smoky Mountains National Park, so they brought some clients to explore the Park and develop a model of a tour that they could offer their clients. "A friend who works in the Park gave the people from Country Walkers my card. They called me, so I met with them and we hiked. During the hike, I did my naturalist thing—talked to the hikers about the plants, birds, animal tracks, anything along the trail they were interested in, and I answered their questions. That was pretty

Starts own guide
business, Outdoor
Adventures

Leads interpretive hikes
for Country Walkers

much my interview. We discussed pay and decided to join forces."

Liz is usually away from her business for six days when she leads a hiking tour for Country Walkers. "I also do other programs where I travel. I go to inns for six days to lead guided

(cardiopulmonary resuscitation, a technique to manually keep a heart attack victim's heart beating and get oxygen into her body). They also have many responsibilities in addition to the hiking. They must arrange for the vans needed to take

The night before a hike, I read my notes about what I've seen on the trail during past hikes—different species of plants and animals, medicinal plants, geology.

hikes during the day and give talks at night. Back-to-back trips can make my schedule pretty tight, but this is all part of making a business work."

There are usually two guides for Country Walkers tours. The guides must be certified in first aid and CPR

the hikers from the inn to the trail and back. The guides work with the innkeeper to arrange times of the meals, and for the lunches carried on the hikes. "We get together to do introductions before the first hike, but people really get to know each other during meals and hiking, when they're more relaxed."

Liz does a lot of preparation for the hikes she leads. "I want to give people as much correct information as possible. I'm a note-taker. The night before a hike, I read my notes about what I've seen on the trail during past hikes—different species of plants and animals, medicinal plants, geology. There's so much that I never run out of information to share with the hikers." For Country Walkers hikes, Liz must make sure that they start on time so they get to their destination and back to the inn on time for dinner and any evening programs. "We have to leave room in the schedule in case someone gets hurt, or maybe we see something that everyone wants to spend time watching." Liz may ask people to stretch to loosen up before and after a hike. She ensures that all of the hikers have the right footwear, which is very important. "I make sure that they have food, water, and outdoor gear to protect them from the weather." Liz always encourages the hikers to ask questions. If some of the

CAREER CHECKLIST ✓

You'll like this job if you ...

Like wildlife, science, cultural history

Like to be outdoors

Like people

Are patient

Pay attention to detail

Want to share your love of wildlife with others

hikers want a shorter or longer version of the planned hike, Liz and the other guide may split the group to accommodate everyone.

Loves Her Work

Liz loves being outdoors and sharing what she knows with people. "My ultimate goal is to educate people about our environment to increase their awareness. Then, maybe, they will become involved in environmental issues at their local and state levels and when they vote." Liz has found that people love to learn through her hikes. "I meet people who get excited and want to learn. It's a fun thing for me to show them the things that are interesting to me." Liz is at her best when she is outdoors. "If I had to meet 100 people in a formal indoor setting, it would be stressful, but I would be completely comfortable doing that on a trail."

Liz loves her work so much that what she does for work is also play. "Anything to do with the outdoors is a joy for me." Although she is not married, and she has no pets because she is gone so much, Liz has many other interests. "I paint, sketch, and draw. I make my own Christmas card each year." Last year Liz was commissioned to do a painting. "That was exciting and a lot of fun." Liz loves music and played guitar when she was a kid. "I quit guitar because I was very into sports." Liz pursues photography both professionally and for personal pleasure.

A Ton of Opportunities

"There is definitely a market for this work. There are a ton of opportuni-

Wealth is not my goal. I don't worry about making lots of money, but I've always been able to support myself.

ties." Besides doing her current work, Liz would like to write letters about her business to schools to offer field trips for the students.

Liz makes a good living from her work. "It's important to know that wealth is not my goal. If you're interested in doing this work, you should not worry about making lots of money, but I've always been able to support myself. When I started my business, I had a savings account because, when you're starting a business, you need financial backing to support yourself." Liz says that she is very frugal—very careful about how she spends her money. "I think that's a quality needed to start a business."

Family Camping Vacations

Liz grew up in a neighborhood on Long Island, New York. She comes from a large family and has six sisters and one brother. "My parents were very family oriented. When we went anywhere or took vacations, we went to parks and camped." Liz believes that her love of the outdoors is an inborn part of her. "My parents nurtured and encouraged me. They never discouraged my love of the outdoors."

In school, Liz liked studying the sciences. "Earth science was a favorite of mine, and biology—anything having to do with plants and animals." Liz also liked to paint and draw. She took a photography class in

high school, and was a member of the Audubon Society.

Liz loved sports. She played Little League softball from ages 7 to 16. She also played field hockey, volleyball, and basketball. "Being from a big family, I was taught to share and be considerate of others. But I think that team sports also help teach these qualities. You learn how to be a member of a team."

Liz chose Cornell University in Ithaca, New York, for undergraduate school. She majored in wildlife science and began doing wildlife research,

which she would do for the next 15 years. "I volunteered for the first research project, then I was hired to do other projects. I love to learn, so I volunteered or worked on different research projects every chance I had."

Liz went on to graduate school, first at Purdue University, then to the University of Florida in Gainesville. She chose Florida because there were a lot of professors who had wildlife and ecology interests similar to hers. During undergraduate and graduate school, Liz volunteered for 4-H where she taught birding classes and took members on birding walks.

Making a Difference

Liz learned an important lesson—that one or a few individuals can make a difference—when she got involved creating a grassroots organization, the Paynes Prairie Wildlife Coalition (PPWC). The group successfully worked with the Florida Department of Transportation, convincing them to build a wildlife eco-passage (an underpass/barrier

system allowing wildlife to travel under a highway). The highway involved cuts across the Paynes Prairie State Preserve and had the distinction of having the highest road kill of any road in the United States. It took four and a half years of positive, persistent effort by group members, but the project was finished in November 2000. "This was such a valuable experience for me. It showed me what one or a few individuals actually could accomplish."

Coming to the Smoky Mountains

After getting her master's degree, Liz got grants for several years so she could continue her research in Florida. In February 1998, the U.S. Geological Survey (USGS) hired her to study the amphibians of the Great Smoky Mountains National Park. This project required some office work, but a big part of it was field-work to obtain data on the types and number of species and the locations of amphibians in the Park.

After she finished the USGS project, Liz wanted to stay near the Park, but she needed another job. "For the first time in my life, I was uncertain about what I would do next. I always knew what I wanted to do, and it just always came along. At this point, I had to really think 'What do I want to do?'" Liz applied for jobs elsewhere. "I was offered a job that was half teaching and half research, but it was located in the Midwest region of the United States, and I didn't want to live there. So I turned the job down and started my own business because I really wanted to be here."

Since moving to the Great Smoky Mountains area, Liz has always lived in Tennessee on the northwest side of the Park. "This location is just amazing."

Catherine Karnow

Catherine Karnow

Photographer, Mill Valley, CA

Twin Majors in Comparative Literature and Semiotics

Photographer

She Shoots People ... and Places

At a young age, Catherine Karnow began wandering by herself around a fishing village near Hong Kong where she lived. She loved the adventure, exploring where her curiosity led her.

"My parents let me be very independent. I'm exactly like I was at age 7. I don't like being told what to do. I love to explore and go beyond boundaries. I'm motivated by curiosity. And I am comfortable being a foreigner, being among people who are different from me."

Catherine is a professional photographer who works free lance, taking assignments from several clients. Some are publishers of travel guidebooks and magazines. Other clients are corporations that want portraits of their people or various photos of their business activities. Catherine

Photographer:

Photographers' earnings vary depending upon the type and amount of work they do.

Beginning photographers working as assistants: Usually start working for no pay, then perhaps $50 to $75 per day, quickly working up to current rates ($150 to $200 per day, more if the project is for advertising).

An established photographer: People who start their own business may not earn any salary in the beginning. They invest their own money in the business, they get more money through loans or venture capital, and, until they make a profit, they probably pay themselves a small salary and put profits back into the business to help it grow. Catherine is running her own business, with 50 percent of her income coming from shoots and 50 percent from sales of her photos. On average she will clear around $150,000.

CATHERINE'S CAREER PATH

**Born and raised
▼ in Hong Kong**

**Gets hooked on
▼ photography in
high school**

**Takes photo trips
▼ to New York City
in teens**

also sells copies of photos she has taken (called her stock photos) to people like art directors who may want a specific type photo, such as a street scene in Vietnam or an elderly man in France.

Based in San Francisco, Catherine runs her business out of her home office. When she is not on assignment, she and her studio manager do the necessary activities—sending out bills, collecting payments, banking, keeping records, selling photos, negotiating terms of assignments, and taking care of equipment.

Occasionally, Catherine has assignments in the San Francisco area. Usually, her photo projects take two to three weeks. Sometimes she can stay at home and travel to the shoot each day. More often she is away from home.

A Typical Travel Assignment

Travel photography assignments—to tell a story about a region or city with photos—can take Catherine anywhere in the world.

"I prepare before I leave and also on the airplane. I know where I'm going and what I'm going to do. I research the area to learn what makes it special. I make a list and am constantly adding and crossing things off."

"When I arrive, I seek out any contacts I may have and ask questions— what's happening, anything new, and I ask about the things I'm planning to shoot. I usually have someone helping—to carry equipment or to translate the language. We meet at my hotel in the morning (sometimes before dawn if I want a sunrise shot).

Then we go all day. Sometimes we go until two or three in the morning if there is night life to shoot. (Some cities, especially in Asia, never 'sleep.') We eat on the run and in the car."

Catherine will take hundreds of rolls of film to create a portrait of a place. She shows the geography (like lakes or mountains) and how these surroundings affect lifestyles. She seeks out the rich people, the poor people, the 'movers and shakers,' and the characters. She covers the food, sports, industries, and agriculture of a place. She shows what a place is known for—maybe it is a famous market or olive trees or fishing. She shows how people work and play.

CATHERINE'S CAREER PATH

Builds freelance business, travels to Europe, Asia

Moves to San Francisco area

"I'll shoot lawn bowling in England or Australia, because it is typical there. But I won't shoot it in San Francisco, where they bowl but it is not typical of the city."

do a lot of writing. I have to produce caption information for the photos, but I also do it for myself. I find when I write about the experience of the shoot it becomes more vivid for me.

For my 15th birthday, my parents built me my own darkroom, and I'd stay there late every night.

To get the photos she wants, Catherine must be bold and aggressive, but at the same time friendly and tuned in to how she is being received by the people she is photographing.

"I have to be very bold, but friendly. A photographer needs good radar, so you can sense whether people are receptive and you can go ahead or whether it is time to turn around and go in another direction."

Catherine must also take notes and keep track of what she is shooting. "I

Later I can develop it into a story to go with the pictures."

Some of these stories Catherine has posted to an online magazine she is part of. "Atlasmagazine.com is a place where a group of illustrators, photographers, and writers set up their own work."

When Catherine returns home, she starts the editing process—going through all her photos, labeling them, and selecting those she will turn in to the client as part of her assignment.

And, of course, she presents her invoice according to the terms she agreed upon—usually a day rate plus expenses for a certain number of days.

It Started in Tenth Grade

The family returned to the United States when Catherine was 12 years old. She was attending a private school for girls in Bethesda, Maryland, close to Washington, DC, when she took her first photography class.

"The teacher, Barbara Hadley, was so enthusiastic, and she was always giving me good feedback about what I was doing. The school had many photography books, which I found inspirational. Within six months I knew I wanted to be a photographer. I took pictures all the time, was the school photographer, and I would create photo projects. I had a little car and some weekends I would drive to New York City and take photos."

Catherine would spend hours in the school darkroom developing her black-and-white photos. "I'd stay at

CAREER CHECKLIST ✓

You'll like this job if you ...

- Can be very bold, move past your fears

- Are motivated by curiosity about people and places

- Seek adventure, love to explore

- Will do research and pay attention to details

- Are comfortable with all types of people

- Can 'rough it' when traveling

In Vietnam with former general of North Vienam army

the school until midnight, everyday, until one day the principal found me there. He had no idea I was there so late every night and couldn't believe my parents would let me. He said I could only stay until 6 p.m. Then, for my 15th birthday, my parents built me my own darkroom, and I'd stay there until midnight."

For her senior-year photo project, Catherine presented a picture story of an old beachside resort town falling apart. "I visited my boyfriend at Princeton and everyday I'd drive to Asbury Park, New Jersey, and take pictures."

Exciting Summers, Then College

During the summers, Catherine got intern jobs. A college friend of her father's was a professional photographer at Magnum Photos in Paris, France. "He had encouraged my parents to encourage me in photography. I got to work at Magnum for one month as an intern. I believe it was because he knew I was serious about being a photographer. It was incredibly exciting to be there."

The next summer she interned at the Sunday *Times* in London, but that was not as exciting because there was not as much for her to do. "Each summer I earned about $100 for the month, and then I'd travel until I ran out of money and had to come home."

his life." She stayed an extra semester plus a month to edit and finish the film. After the film premiered February 1984 at the Berlin Film Festival, Catherine went to Paris to live.

I show what a place is known for—maybe it is a famous market or olive trees or fishing.

Catherine wanted a liberal arts education because she was interested in subjects like literature, anthropology, and languages. "My parents grilled into me that a good education could open doors for me and that I should take this time in my life to learn." She chose Brown University and took courses in filmmaking at nearby Rhode Island School of Design.

"My last two years of school I became very serious about filmmaking. I watched films and made films." Catherine made a 30-minute, black-and-white film called *Brooklyn Bridge*. "I wrote the script, directed and filmed it with three of my friends. It was about an adult man who lived with his mother, about the last day of

"I had some contacts there, I spoke French, and I wanted to live in a foreign country. I was open to any job in film or still photography, but it was difficult to get work. I took lots of pictures to build up my portfolio to show my work."

Impatient and feeling unproductive, Catherine decided she preferred the freedom of still photography—filmmaking involved so many people and less independent action within projects. She returned to her family in the Washington, DC, area and began free lance work as a photographer's assistant. This is a common route for getting paid while learning about professional photography.

Building a Reputation

Catherine's first paid travel project came "through word of mouth, a friend of a friend. A guidebook editor, who was looking for someone to do a book on France, had spoken with a college friend who remembered my work in college and suggested the editor contact me. While in Paris I had shot a set of photos about wine. When the editor saw my pictures, she hired me."

Catherine went to France, bought a car, and drove all over the country. Then she came back and helped put together the book. "Though I didn't make any money (the $10,000 fee all went for expenses), I ended up with a nice set of photos to show, which is very important."

Returning home with zero money, Catherine started assisting again. Her next break came when an art director of a design agency—after seeing a handful of photos she'd taken in France—hired her to do travel portraits of areas in the Northeast United States. These appeared in the front pages of local telephone books.

Catherine began to get other clients. "In 1989 I did a coffee table book on Scotch whisky. I traveled to

In Bombay

Scotland in the summer and fall. I took pictures of not only the pubs, distilleries, and whisky shops, but the landscapes, the fishing, hunting, the lifestyle of whisky. It was a nostalgic look at Scotland."

As the number of clients and travel photo projects increased, Catherine realized she could live most anywhere and still do her work. In 1992, she chose to move to San Francisco. "I love this area. It's wonderful to be paid to photograph places like Big Sur."

Today Catherine's work appears in the magazines *National Geographic*, *National Geographic Traveler*, *Smithsonian*, and the French and German *GEO*. Her book projects include *Passage to Vietnam, Women in the Material World,* and the *Day in the Life* series. When she is not working, she enjoys visiting family and friends, going to photo shows and symphony concerts, and just relaxing at home.

GROUNDBREAKERS
Photographers

Laura Gilpin (1891-1979) is known as an American landscape photographer, but she was both a commercial and a fine art photographer.

Laura began taking photographs while a teenager in Colorado. As a free-thinking westerner, she portrayed the landscape as a historical backdrop for the relationship between the environment and the people who live within it. She produced works that documented a region and examined it in a historical and cultural context. Her work was published in five major books; the final book, *The Enduring Navaho*, was her masterpiece.

Margaret Bourke-White (1904 or 1906-1971) achieved many "firsts" and published several photography books. In 1930, she was the first Western photographer allowed into the Soviet Union, and years later she was the only foreign photographer in the Soviet Union when the Germans attacked Moscow. She traveled the world on photography assignments for *Life* magazine. She was the first woman the U.S. Army accredited as a war correspondent in World War II, and one of the first photographers to enter and document the death camps. *Life* published her photos, and *The Living Dead of Buchenwald* became a classic.

One of her famous photos featured black victims of a flood standing in a breadline beneath a billboard of a smiling white family in a car. The board's headline read "World's Highest Standard of Living. There's no way like the American Way." Another famous photo was *Gandhi at his Spinning Wheel*. Her autobiography is *Portrait of Myself*.

Sources: women in the visual arts; www.distinguished-women.com/biographies/bourke-white.html

Donna Clucky

Donna Clucky

Travel Agent, American Automobile Association, Hendersonville, NC

Travel Agent

Travel Services with Attention to Details

Donna never applied for her current job. She was working part-time at a travel agency, when she got a call from the manager of the American Automobile Association (AAA)—a large, national travel company that offers membership to automobile owners and travel agent services to the public. She talked with Donna about working for AAA in nearby Asheville, North Carolina. "That office was on the other side of town from where I was working. I told her that I was as far north of Hendersonville (where Donna lives) as I wanted to be. I told her I would think about working in their Hendersonville office." Three weeks later, she offered Donna a job in the Hendersonville office at a dollar more than her then hourly wage. "I said, 'O.K.!'" Donna worked part-time

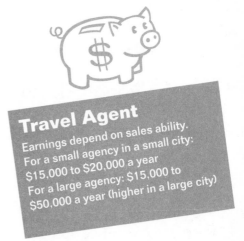

Travel Agent

Earnings depend on sales ability.
For a small agency in a small city: $15,000 to $20,000 a year
For a large agency: $15,000 to $50,000 a year (higher in a large city)

DONNA'S CAREER PATH

Wants to be
▼ nurse as child

Leaves college,
▼ becomes secretary

Marries
▼ Jerry, moves
to Wisconsin

during her first two years, earning about the same as her previous job.

Donna is now a full-time travel agent for the Hendersonville office. "We do travel packages for members office. She works Monday through Friday, usually from 8:30 a.m. to 5:30 p.m. "The mornings start slow, but by 10 a.m. it's very busy. Mondays and Fridays are the busiest. Tuesdays

If you make a mistake, you've lost a client.

People do not tolerate mistakes.

and nonmembers. I can't say enough about the quality of the job. Most travel companies are small and don't provide benefits to their travel agents because they can't afford to. AAA is supportive, they train us constantly, they compensate us well, and they provide benefits."

Full Days

Donna has been at her job for four years. She lives five minutes from her through Thursdays we try to catch up. We're on the phone all the time. We're very automated; we do everything by email and the Internet. We're trying to get customers to use more email."

Donna's office has four travel agents. "Everybody does everything. We all answer phones. We all help our clients get information for road trips and with membership, insurance, everything. We're very customer oriented. If a client stops by when I'm leaving for lunch, I stay to help her.

Travels with Jerry on
▼ business trips

Has daughter, moves
▼ to Arizona

Becomes
▼ business
travel agent

We never go home at the end of the day without returning a phone call, no matter how late it is."

"The longer you're working, the more you build your client contacts, people who travel a lot and who will recommend you to others." Donna listens to what her clients want and develops travel packages for vacations all over the world that include air travel, rail travel, hotel, tours, and local transportation. She does cruises for them, too.

"There are two keys to being a good agent. One, you must be courteous and outgoing so people know you care about what they want and that you respect them. This is how you sell any

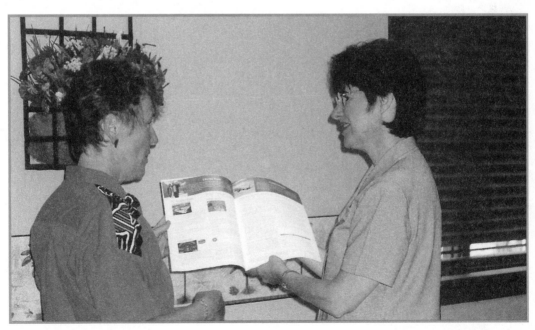

Moves to North
Carolina, does
leisure travel

Accepts job with AAA
Hendersonville office

product. Two, you must also be very detail oriented—fast but thorough and accurate. If you make a mistake, you've lost a client. People do not tolerate mistakes." Details include accounting functions like tracking payments due to companies that sell the products you need for your client's trip (car rental, hotel, rail, etc.), ensuring all travel documents are present and correct, and advising clients about passport and visa requirements. Computer skills needed to address these details include word processing, spreadsheet, email, and Internet searches. "We're not doing a trip that just gets by, we strive to do the perfect trip."

Donna keeps a file of her clients' trips and interests and follows up with them to see how their trip went. "I listen to all of their pros and cons. It's another way to learn." Donna also contacts them if she learns of a trip they might be interested in.

Learning a Big Part of the Job

All travel agents must keep up to date about the various travel packages (called products) that their

You really need to know and experience something to sell it. The only way you're going to really know a place is to travel there.

agency offers. At a large company, agents attend special training classes and trade shows on a regular basis. If you work for a small agency, some of the tour/cruise company representatives will visit occasionally and tell you what you need to know about their company. "There are so many different companies that you can sell, and you need to know all the details of each one of them. In addition to this, you will need extensive computer training for different programs and Internet booking sites. It takes real dedication to on-going learning on a monthly basis throughout your career."

Travel Experience the Key

A benefit of being a travel agent is low-cost travel. "However, we can't travel too often because we're supposed to be at work selling travel to others." Traveling is key to a travel agent's growth. "You really need to know and love something to have confidence in selling it. The only way you're going to know a place and

CAREER CHECKLIST ✓

You'll like this job if you ...

Love to travel

Are outgoing and care about people

Are a good listener, understand people's wants and needs

Are detail oriented

Are computer oriented

Are enthusiastic about learning new things

Are confident

whether you love it is to travel there." Donna got her opportunity to travel when she married a man whose work demanded lots of travel. They met in Chicago, where Donna grew up.

"I was a quiet child. I loved medical television shows and wanted to be a nurse, but my parents wanted me to be teacher." Donna enrolled in college as an education major but had dropped out because the cost was too burdensome for her parents. "I was a secretary working at an equipment company when I met my husband, Jerry."

Donna traveled with her husband throughout the United States, including Alaska and Hawaii. They've also been to many Caribbean islands and to places in Mexico. When Donna had their daughter, Amanda, she stayed home for a while. "When I went back to work, I got another secretarial job. It was good for me, but you can only advance so far."

When the family moved to Phoenix, Arizona, Donna's effort to help Jerry launched her into her travel career. "We have a close relationship and always try to help each other. Since I didn't have another job, I did whatever I could to make his life easier because Jerry's travel schedule was horrendous. He couldn't find a travel agent to keep up with him, keeping track of the plane and hotel and car rental arrangements which could change every day. I went to a Phoenix travel agency, explained the situation to the owner, and asked her if I could be an outside agent for my husband. She said 'No problem.'"

The owner advised Donna that she didn't need to go to school to be a travel agent. "That was a mistake. You need to go to school if you want to be good." But because Donna did only corporate/business travel for her husband, she did the job without going to school. "She sent me to school to learn the computer system. That was enough for many years."

When Jerry's job took the family to Hendersonville, Donna got into leisure/vacation travel, "a different work experience and travel that I did not need to go to school. He suggested a geography class. When I started working, there wasn't time for it. But I believe if you want to be a successful travel agent, you need an outgoing personality plus a two-year degree in travel."

Now that Jerry doesn't have to travel much for his job, he is more interested in traveling for vacations.

> I don't think this job is as much about having a talent for sales as it is having a love for travel. I'm a quiet person, but I come alive about anything concerning travel.

world from corporate travel. I enjoy leisure travel much more than corporate, but you really need an education to do it."

Seeking advice, Donna talked to the Travel and Tourism Department head at Blue Ridge Community College nearby. "He said I had so much "We try to take two vacations a year, and we like to do one cruise." What Donna likes best about traveling is "seeing the different scenery and learning about different cultures."

"I don't think this job is as much about having a talent for sales as it is having a love for travel. I'm a quiet person, but I come alive about anything concerning travel."

While travel is a big part of Donna's life, she also likes to sew, and she and Jerry enjoy camping and boating. Three grandchildren keep them busy.

The Business is Changing

For travel agents, the office procedures have become more automated,

better fare than the Internet. People also like personal service. They want to know if a destination is interesting and fun, if a certain hotel is good. They want customer service when they pay for a travel package."

Donna believes that small travel agencies and the Internet can't provide the same service and value that a large agency can. "AAA hosts tour talks, cruise nights, high teas, and other events all year to promote

I enjoy leisure travel much more than corporate, but you really need an education to do it.

which means agencies need fewer agents to do the work. Agents now focus less on air tickets and more on cruises and tours. (The airlines stopped paying agencies for selling tickets.) "AAA gets no commission on airline tickets, but we charge a service fee." Donna doesn't think that travel services on the Internet, like Expedia.com and Orbiz.com, have hurt them. "I think we usually give a

travel sales. AAA has a lot of buying power and incentives that small agencies can't offer, like shipboard credits that you use like money to buy things on the ship, upgrades on cruises, and low-cost insurance. Most of the time, you don't have to be a member to get them."

Large agencies like AAA operate differently from small agencies, so their agents usually make more money and have benefits. "Commissions are based on volume of sales, so the larger the company, the more market share it has, and the higher the commissions go. I believe that, eventually, there won't be many small, independent travel agencies. The large agencies, Internet and cruise-only companies will drive them out of business, just like the large superstores drive the small, independent stores out of business." Donna notes that this is especially true in small cities. "In areas where there aren't enough people who use agencies, the sales volume is low and so agents don't earn a decent wage."

AAA pays an hourly wage and provides benefits. "Our wage is based on the amount of sales we have for the year. With 1,000 offices, we have a lot of sales power, so the sky's the limit. It all depends on how aggressively we pursue sales." Donna says this is good but can also be bad. "You sometimes tend to drive yourself too hard and wear yourself out."

GROUNDBREAKERS
Pistol-Packing Mary's Café

Mary Fields (1832-1914) was born a slave in Tennessee. She grew up an orphan, living by her wits and her strength. She traveled to Toledo, Ohio, and worked for a Catholic convent, where she formed a strong bond with Mother Amadeus.

When the nuns moved to Montana and Mary learned that Mother Amadeus was ill, she went west to be with them. Mary nursed her back to health and stayed to help build the mission school. She was a pistol-packing, hard-drinking woman, who needed no help in the task she took on, protecting the nuns. But she was turned away from the mission because of her behavior. Then the nuns financed her in business and she opened a café. Mary's business didn't do well because of her big heart—she would feed the hungry for free.

In 1895 she got a job as a U.S. mail coach driver for the Cascade County region of central Montana. She became known as "Stagecoach" Mary. She and her mule Moses never missed a day.

Source: www.lkwdpl.org/wihohio/fiel-mar.htm

Karen Cure
Karen Cure

Editorial Director and Vice President, Fodor's Travel
Publications, New York, NY

Major, English

Travel Writer
and Editor

She Guides Guidebook Writers

Karen Cure travels from Hastings, New York, to her job in New York City at Fodor's Travel Publications, a company that publishes guidebooks for travel destinations all over the world. As Fodor's editorial director, Karen's job is to "set into motion the things everyone else does." Karen manages a staff of 22. There are four senior editors who report to Karen and 18 editors and assistants who report to the senior editors.

The Journey to Fodor's

Before she became Fodor's editorial director, Karen logged many miles during her 15 years as a freelance travel writer. Her travel-writing career took her on exciting adventures to places all over the world—to Asia, Europe, and throughout the United

Travel Writer

Depends upon region. These are salaries in a big city and include benefits such as health insurance, vacation, savings or pension funds.

Editorial Assistant: $30,000

Editorial Director: $74,000 to $150,000

Freelance travel writing: People who start their own business may not earn any salary in the beginning. They invest their own money in the business, they get more money through loans or venture capital, and they probably pay themselves a small salary and put profits back into the business to help it grow. Karen's earnings ranged from $15,000 to $45,000.

KAREN'S CAREER PATH

Loves to read and sew as a girl

Travels to France, Ireland during high school, college

Takes job as secretary at Curtis

States. Whether downhill skiing in Japan and Switzerland or rafting in West Virginia, she wrote about her travels and gave her opinions about the places she visited. How she became a freelance travel writer is a journey in itself.

First Taste of Travel

Karen had her first travel experience when she was a high school sophomore. "I went to a small town in France through Indiana University's honors program for foreign language students. Hundreds of kids applied, but just 30 were chosen. We went to school all day and didn't speak English the whole summer. I had trouble speaking English when I first came back."

Karen traveled to Ireland through another study program after her sophomore year in college. "By the time I graduated from Brown University in Rhode Island, in 1971, I knew I loved to travel and was good at writing, and being a travel writer seemed like a natural career for me."

Karen got advice from a travel writer her father knew. "He said most travel writers are freelance (they are self-employed and sell their writing to various businesses). The best way to pursue a freelance travel-writing career is to work full time for a publisher, because you need a steady job to pay the bills. You build your freelance career by moonlighting (doing your writing after you've left your job for the day)." Karen, who went home to Indianapolis, Indiana, right after graduation, decided she wanted to return to New England to work on a small-town newspaper while building

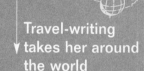
her freelance travel-writing career. "But I needed money to live on while I looked for this newspaper job, so I needed another job just to save money to do that."

It was hard to get a job in 1971. "The only job I could get was being the secretary to the secretary of the editor-in-chief at the Curtis Publishing Company, which had just moved to Indiana." Curtis published magazines such as *The Saturday Evening Post* and *Jack and Jill*, a children's magazine. Another Curtis magazine, *Holiday*, was based in New York City. When Curtis closed the office there and hired a new staff in Indiana, Karen became associate editor. She began writing for *Holiday* and doing press trips. (A travel destination that wants to promote itself invites a group of writers and shows them around the place in hopes they will write articles about it in their publications.)

"I met an editor from *Better Homes and Gardens* who gave me a chance to write for them. It was my lucky break.

KAREN'S CAREER PATH

Marries, hired as Fodor's executive editor

Promoted to Fodor's editorial director

Soon, I was getting lots of paid assignments from *Better Homes and Gardens*. In 1973, I quit my job at *Holiday*. Now I was a freelance travel writer, and I decided to move to New York because that's where I had always really wanted to live. I had a lot of assignments that I researched and wrote on my drive to New York."

Karen shared an apartment with a college friend during that first summer. Then she moved into the Barbizon Hotel for Women. (Now a standard hotel, the Barbizon used to be a hotel for women only. It provided a safe, affordable place to stay.) After working a while, she was able to rent her own apartment.

In 1984, while on a press trip for a travel publication, Karen met an editor who introduced her to Stephen Birnbaum, the editor-in-chief of *Diversion*, a travel magazine for physi-cians. "I did a lot of work for this magazine. When Steve started his own guidebooks, I also wrote for them." During another press trip, Karen met Mike Spring. They became friends, since Mike, an editor at *Scholastic* then, really wanted to work on travel guidebooks as well. Later, when Mike started working as

> **By the time I graduated from college I knew I loved to travel and was good at writing, so I wanted to be a travel writer.**

an editorial director at Fodor's, "he'd call me when he needed to hire people and I would suggest someone I thought might be suitable. For example, when Mike was looking for someone to be managing editor at Fodor's, I gave him the name of a woman I had worked with at Birnbaum Travel Guides—Denise Degennaro. She's still there. The funny thing is that when Mike was looking for a executive editor, Denise thought of me."

That was in 1992, and then Karen married. She met her husband, Bennett Fradkin, an architect, through a friend. But it wasn't until she decided to fix up her apartment and contacted Bennett for help that the two got together. "We had a great time working on my renovation. I invited him to my 33rd birthday party, and that was it." They got married and Karen decided to spend less time traveling.

When she became executive editor, Karen's boss was her old friend Mike. The biggest part of her job was to meet weekly with each editor to discuss assigned books. "I needed to know whether they had assigned the book

CAREER CHECKLIST ✓

You'll like this job if you ...

- Are adventurous, like to explore the unknown

- Like to write, read, and learn

- Enjoy travel, can cope with different cultures

- Are friendly, meet and get to know people easily

- Are good at meeting deadlines

- Are detail oriented

- Can form and express your opinions

- Can manage your money

to a writer, whether the book was written, what the story was, whether they were editing the book, and had it gone to copyediting. There were always editorial issues. For example, for Fodor's format we always provide an exact street address with a street number and a street name. However, some countries, like Portugal, are pretty casual about using street numbers, so the writer doesn't always gather them. I would talk to the editor to figure out what to do. Was the writer just lazy or were there truly no street numbers? We had to figure out how to handle these situations so the books would be as consistent with Fodor's format as possible."

Editorial Director and Media Spokesperson

In 1995, Mike left Fodor's. Karen was promoted to his job, editorial director. During 1997, her job included working as a Fodor's spokesperson to the media. (Media included television, radio, newspapers, and magazines.) "Fodor's has a publicity department, but the media usually want someone other than a publicity person to be a spokesperson."

Being a media spokesperson meant that Karen appeared on television and radio, was interviewed by various TV and radio talk-show hosts, and went to bookstores to talk about Fodor's guidebooks. To do this work, Karen took training sessions about how to speak and act on television and radio and how to handle interviews with newspaper and magazine reporters. "It's not easy to get your message across to the media. I enjoyed the bookstore appearances because I got to talk with the readers, which I rarely get to do." Karen has been on ABC's "Good Morning, America," and she's been quoted in *Newsweek* magazine, *USA Today*, and *The New York Times*.

Taking Care of Business

On a typical workday, Karen, like many executives, oversees ongoing projects and goes to meetings. "On Tuesdays, I meet with my senior editors. We think ahead to see what documents our staff might need to do their job and what decisions must be made. We try to keep all of the guidebooks similar. This means we must decide on a policy for all of the books and communicate that policy to everyone." For example, the way Fodor's organizes a guidebook (listing the area's history, culture, geography, major cities, industries, and special items of interest to travelers) makes all the

managing editor, her old friend Denise. "I get a lot of information from them that I must communicate to my senior editors. If we decide to do a new book, I may assign it to an editor or plan the book far enough ahead myself to launch it. I'm very involved in the beginning of book writing. I'm interested in editing, but that's not really my job; that's my hobby."

Karen rarely edits the guidebooks herself, unless one needs special at-

The only way to understand about writing is to write a lot and read.

books similar and easy for their readers to use. As an executive, it's also Karen's job to answer the senior editors' questions and brainstorm solutions to any problems. She must talk with other Fodor's department heads when her staff needs something from them to do their job. "I spend the whole week taking care of issues generated by this meeting."

On Wednesdays, Karen meets with her immediate supervisor and Fodor's

tention. "Right now, I'm editing a book that was written by a packager, a small company that creates books for many large publishing houses. I'm working to organize the book better, add new information, and make the language clearer. My staff is brainstorming extra ideas for hints and tips to put in. I've done my editing on the page proofs; next, I'll keyboard my edits into the computer file.

Karen doesn't talk to writers too

often. But, she says, "I know about many of them because I'm interested in what they do. Since being at Fodor's, one policy that I'm responsible for is that we always use writers who live in the destinations they're writing about. I keep track of who's doing what to make sure that they are doing that." When a writer stops by unannounced and the editor working with him is unavailable, Karen may meet with the writer herself. Still, she fields a few calls a week from writers who have sent letters proposing new books. She talks to them and usually asks to see writing samples. "How a person writes is just as important as what he or she wants to write about."

Taking Care of Family

Karen and Bennett have two daughters—Becky, in fifth grade, and Sara, in sixth grade. Most days they leave home at 8:20 a.m., drop off the girls at middle school, then drive to the station and take the train into Manhattan.

After work, the girls and their babysitter meet Karen's train at 6:30 p.m. Karen takes the sitter home and

then goes home to help her daughters with homework. "I don't have much time to watch TV. I go to bed at 10:15." Karen and Bennett believe in sports for their daughters. "We grew up in nonsporting families." Becky is on a swim team, and Sara is a gymnast. Karen and Bennett share responsibility for getting the girls to their meets. When both girls have sports activities, Karen doesn't have to be home until 9:00 p.m., so she takes advantage of this time to work late. "Sometimes, when I take Becky swimming, I take a laptop computer with me and go to a nearby bookstore to do some work." Karen doesn't usually work on weekends.

Her Grandmother's Influence

One of Karen's grandmothers was a teacher. "She spent a lot of time with us and taught me how to read and sew, which I loved to do as a child." Whenever she visited her grandmothers, Karen would go to the town library and check out a tall stack of books. "My brother would play, and I would read. This was my idea of a great week." Karen took piano lessons, which she hated. "My parents finally let me quit when I was in the ninth grade."

Karen's father was a doctor. "I was interested in being a doctor, but my parents told me that a woman could not be a doctor because it was incompatible with raising a family, which was the destiny of all women back when I was a kid."

Karen has several hobbies that she manages to work into her busy life. She and her family go to Cape Cod every summer. She likes to read cookbooks and cook, and she still sews, making elaborate Halloween costumes with satin, lace, and all kinds of amazing glittery fabrics. She is taking piano lessons again. "Now I'm really thanking my parents for making me take them as long as I did."

Ginifer Maceau

Ginifer Maceau

Programs Manager, Homestead Ranch, Matfield Green, KS

Major, English

Guest Ranch
Programs Manager

Guests Learn Horse Sense at Prairie Ranch

My parents said the first word I ever spoke wasn't *mommy* or *daddy*; it was *horsy*." So it's not surprising that Ginifer Maceau became programs manager responsible for the guest programs at the Homestead Ranch in Matfield Green, Kansas.

When Ginifer got involved in the Homestead Ranch's guest programs, she expanded them to run year-round. In the spring and fall, the Prairie Women Adventures program gives women the opportunity to learn how to be cowhands by participating in the activities of a working cattle ranch. During the time when cows have calves, they ride the herd to check whether cows or calves are in trouble. They help out at branding cattle and burning pastures. There are also wildflower programs and

Guest Ranch Program Manager

People who start their own business may not earn any salary in the beginning. They invest their own money in the business, they get more money through loans or venture capital, and, until they make a profit or "go public" by selling stock, they probably pay themselves a small salary and put profits back into the business to help it grow.

Owns and rides champion jumper as girl

Graduates college, owns horse wherever she goes

Works in advertising, fundraising

horse programs. "Someone asked why we don't include men. The bunkhouse is like a dormitory, so we don't ask women to share their space with men they don't know."

Ginifer developed Prairie Youth Adventures—week-long riding camps for young people. They run five weeks during the summer, three weeks for girls and two weeks for boys.

The Bunkhouse Rental program is for families, businesses, and other groups that rent the entire bunkhouse for reunions, conferences, retreats. An artist uses the bunkhouse to conduct a painting workshop twice a year. "When there are men and women in the bunkhouse, they know up front that they'll be sharing the same space."

Ginifer is involved in all programs dealing with horses and is primarily responsible for the Trail Riding Program. Jane Koger, the ranch's owner, is primarily involved with the activities that include cattle.

What She Really Wanted to Do

Ginifer had lots of interesting jobs in some great cities before going to the Homestead Ranch. "All the time I was working in these places, I wanted to start a riding camp for problem adolescents. When I was young, I participated in a program for the juvenile (correctional) system while living in Cedar Rapids, Iowa. Put kids with a horse and it's a great equalizer. I loved it." However, while working at a behavioral health agency in Phoenix, Arizona, Ginifer realized that if she started such a program, "I would have to deal with

Helps friend with
behavioral health
agency

Visits Homestead
Ranch, meets owner
Jane Koger

Proposes
summer riding
camp at ranch

the state bureaucracy and become an administrator. I didn't want that."

A friend in Kansas City told Ginifer about Jane Koger and her Homestead Ranch. "He told me I really needed to see this ranch in Kansas. I kept responding, 'If I want to go to a ranch, I'll go to my college roommate's ranches in Wyoming and Arizona. Why would I want to go to Kansas?'" When he agreed to pay her way, Ginifer went to Kansas in the fall of 1997 and met Jane.

"Jane is a cow person; she's not a horse person." Jane was doing her programs six weekends a year. She was looking for a someone to do the horse programs. "The guests always want to

ride." Ginifer told Jane about her dressage (guiding horses through complex maneuvers) and jumping background. Jane asked her if she would like to do the horse programs. "I told her I would love to, but I would need to make a liv-

riding camp. She called Jane with an idea. "Jane wasn't doing anything on the ranch during the summer. I asked her how she felt about doing a riding camp for kids and she said she'd think about it." Jane called Ginifer the next

> I have to take care of the horses twice a day, every-day. When you're building a business, you're pretty much doing all the work yourself.

ing until the program got up and running. I didn't know how I would do this in a rural area." So Ginifer went home to Phoenix.

"When I got home, I saw that my friends were sending their kids to volleyball and soccer camps for $800 a week." Ginifer realized that parents would pay well to send their kids to

day. "She said I could use her horses, her bunkhouse, and her land if I gave her a business plan." Ginifer drew on her past experience to develop the business plan. Jane liked it.

"I went to the ranch so we could discuss everything before I made this life-changing move. I wanted to be sure I wasn't making a big mistake."

Ginifer found that she and Jane worked well together, so she moved to Kansas that summer. "It was too late to do the riding camp that year, so I helped with the Prairie Women Adventures programs. It also gave me time to market and promote the horse programs for the next year."

"Later that year Jane told me she didn't want to do this anymore. I asked her why. I explained that I couldn't have the branding and calving programs without her because she owned the cows." Jane explained that she didn't want to do the business part of the guest programs anymore. "She said if I wanted it, it was mine." So Ginifer and Jane developed a second business plan to reorganize the guest programs, with Ginifer taking over the programs manager position. Ginifer has "wonderful neighbors" who help her out with things like fencing, well houses, and pumps.

A Day on the Ranch

Ginifer notes that horses require more attention than many other ani-

CAREER CHECKLIST ✓

You'll like this job if you ...

Love animals, will care for them

Like meeting new people, can 'read' people

Don't mind hard work, including paperwork

Like the outdoors

Like to tell stories

Have a sense of humor

Are adventurous

morning barn chores after a continental breakfast. Since the bunkhouse is five and a half miles from the horse barn, the guests have an enjoyable drive through country, see wildlife such as bald eagles, turkey buzzards, hawks, deer, and coyotes on the way. After chores, Ginifer demonstrates how she handles her horse so the guests know what the goal of their experience is. "I want to teach them how to read a horse." Ginifer decides which horse each guest will have during their stay.

After the guests have gotten familiar with the horses, they have lunch. After lunch, they ride horses all afternoon.

Each guest catches the horse she's going to ride and saddles and bridles it. Ginifer thinks this involvement helps the guests respect the horses. "I get a lot of people for whom this is their first experience with horses. They need to know that these are big animals and things can go wrong. I sometimes get concerned about some of the riders, but I've never had a problem." Riders must sign a release,

mals. "I have to take care of the horses twice a day, everyday." There is paperwork involved in every business. "I do the administrative work whenever I can. It's hard to do it all by yourself, and when you're building a business, you're pretty much doing it all by yourself." Ginifer arranges for local people to help with cleaning chores and cooking for the guests.

When guests are at the ranch for a horse program, they help with the which means they ride at their own risk and will not hold the ranch and/or business responsible if there is a problem. She has safety helmets for everyone. "Anyone over 21 can refuse the helmet if she initials the release, but I've had very few people decline a helmet." Ginifer convinces them that they want to be wearing a helmet if they fall off the horse in the flint rocks. She takes no chances. "If I don't freedom of being able to ride side-by-side, talking and getting to know each other. We don't follow a trail, we just ride across the prairie and experience the changing land of flint hills and streams and wildlife." When Ginifer has a big group of guests, a former student helps her. "She's my second pair of eyes."

After the ride, the guests take care of their horses, water and feed them.

I developed the Prairie Youth Adventures—week-long riding camps for young people.

have enough solid horses—horses that have learned to behave well with new riders—to accommodate everyone who wants to attend a program, I have to turn guests away." She says that summer's hot weather tends to slow the horses and make them easier to handle.

Ginifer's horses are ranch horses, not trail horses. "So they don't go in a head-to-tail line. Guests enjoy the

Dinner at the bunkhouse is at 8 p.m. "The guests are amazed at how good the food is. They eat well." While the guests enjoy the hot tub after dinner, Ginifer goes home to her trailer by the horse barn. Now it's around 10:30 p.m., and she bakes some desserts or muffins for the next day's meals.

Because she is still getting her business going, Ginifer has a part-time job as hostess and bartender at the Grand Central Hotel in Cottonwood Falls. It takes 45 minutes to drive there, so she must plan her time carefully for her 5 p.m. to 9 p.m. shift. Most of Ginifer's programs run

horses. "I fell in love with a five-gaited, three-year-old mare. I wanted her desperately. They wanted $20,000 for her." Ginifer's father wouldn't buy this horse, but he told Ginifer she

Don't ignore the people skills for the horse skills because they are tied together.

Thursday through Sunday, so she's free for the job the remaining days.

Born a Horse Woman

Ginifer was born in Milwaukee, Wisconsin. She has one brother and one sister. Her father played football for the Cleveland Browns. "My dad took me to the Washington Park Zoo every Sunday to ride the ponies, round and round in circles, for hours." She began riding three-gaited and five-gaited horses in grade school. (A gait-like trot or gallop is how a horse moves by lifting its feet in a particular order or rhythm.) Ginifer also learned to jump

could get a horse when they moved to Cedar Rapids, Iowa.

In Iowa, Ginifer found a three-year-old thoroughbred at a deserted race track "that I had to have because he could jump the moon. He ended up a champion jumper in five states." After Ginifer graduated parochial school, her horse went to college with her at St Norbert College in De Pere, Wisconsin, for three years and Saint Louis University in St. Louis, Missouri, from which she graduated with her area of concentration in English. "I really wanted to be a veterinarian, but back then they accepted, maybe, one female per vet-school class, so it was discouraging." Ginifer attended law school for one year.

Her Horse Moves with Her

Ginifer got her first job as an administrative assistant in Ohio. "They also raised thoroughbreds for the track. My office overlooked the horses." Ginifer also showed horses while living there.

Next, Ginifer worked in advertising and promotion at the Green Bay Visitor and Convention Bureau in Green Bay, Wisconsin. "One of my projects was to build the Green Bay Packers' Hall of Fame, so everybody saw me as a fundraiser instead of doing advertising and promotion. That's how I ended up in fundraising."

Ginifer's fundraising jobs took her to Ft. Collins, Colorado, where she stayed for 15 years, then Denver, Colorado; Cincinnati, Ohio; and Florida State University in Tallahassee. When Ginifer's friend in Phoenix called her to ask for help with some union issues in her behavioral health agency, Ginifer moved there. "We were successful. This work was an interesting learning experience." No matter where Ginifer's jobs took her, she always had a horse.

A Day Off

Ginifer has never married. "I would have been a totally different person if I had married." She has 10 horses, 2 dogs, and 24 barn cats, so she doesn't have much leisure time. "I've been off the ranch twice since I got here. It's hard to find someone to take care of everything. I traveled a lot when I was younger. It's good to stay home now. My fantasy is for someone to do the chores for just one day." In spite of all the work, Ginifer is happy because the guest programs are doing well. "I've had an increase every year. This year I'm starting to pay back the bank loans I needed for the first few years. That's good news."

Lynn Jason

Lynn Jason

Concierge, Ritz-Carlton Hotel, Washington, DC

Hotel Concierge

She Helps Guests Enjoy Their Washington Visit

Lynn Jason works in a really "ritzy" place in Washington, DC—an elegant hotel called the Ritz-Carlton. Her desk sits in the main lobby so it is easy for guests to find. Lynn's title is Concierge, a French word, probably originally meaning a fellow servant or slave. Her job is to provide services that guests ask for—like getting dinner reservations at local restaurants, arranging for tickets to performances, and explaining about Washington's places of interest. She is there to answer questions and fill requests for help and information.

"All the rooms have a button that says 'Concierge.' I get requests for everything from 'Where is a good Thai restaurant?' to 'How do I get to the White House?'" For Lynn to do her job well, she must know all about the city

Concierge
For convention hotels like Hyatt, Omni Shoreham, Ritz-Carlton: $9 to $13 per hour plus tips, also commissions from tour companies and transportation providers.

LYNN'S CAREER PATH

Loves math, science, Girl Scouts	Mother dies, cares for brothers	Works for company that runs hotels

and surrounding area. "I don't have to know everything, but I must know how to get the information—whom to call or what source to check. I'm never afraid to say 'I don't know,' and I follow that immediately with 'I'll find out.'"

Many guests ask Lynn for directions. Lynn has found that getting directions from the guest's destination is the best way to get accurate directions. For example, she calls the restaurant to get directions for getting there from the hotel. "Guests who get lost call me, and I get them back to the hotel." Before guests leave her desk, Lynn asks if they know how to use Washington's Metro (subway), and if not she carefully explains.

Knowing What People Need

Lynn's job requires that she be intuitive—pick up on guests' needs when they may not know themselves. "The Ritz-Carlton wants us to meet and exceed even the unexpressed wishes of our guests. When a guest says he needs transportation from the airport to the hotel, I ask him when he will leave Washington so I can book him round-trip transportation.

I'm never afraid to say "I don't know," and I follow that immediately with "I'll find out." I have to know how to get the information.

Marries, moves to
▼ Washington, DC,
area

Works in husband's
▼ office, has four
children

Divorces,
▼ studies hospitality
management

CONCIERGE

When a guest wants theater tickets, I ask her if she wants dinner reservations."

"When people are impatient and want the information immediately, I tell them 'I want to be sure to give you the correct information,' then they'll usually wait." Upset guests come to the concierge with their problems. "Sometimes I can't fix the problem, but I can listen and sympathize." Lynn helps guests when they are injured or ill. "People are especially nervous when they're ill and are from out of town." Lynn gets doctors and medicine for these guests and helps them get to a hospital, if necessary.

LYNN'S CAREER PATH

Works for
Hyatt, decides
on concierge work

Concierge at Omni
Shoreham, then
Ritz-Carlton

She also takes care of things like making sure that guests get their packages and faxes. She helps them find lost luggage. "I'm good at recovering lost cell phones from cabs."

Some guests are difficult to please. "Secret shoppers are people from ployees can be suspended if they rate poorly. When I have a very demanding guest, I pretend that he is a secret shopper so I won't lose my composure."

One evening, a guest asked Lynn how to get to a certain restaurant. "I

Sometimes you don't know by someone's name or face who's important, so I treat everybody like they're a VIP (very important person).

travel organizations like the American Automobile Association, and even from the hotel itself, who test all of the hotel's departments. They rate the hotel for travelers and provide the hotel with a report. They are intentionally demanding to see how the hotel staff responds. Hotel em- asked him if he had reservations. He said the restaurant didn't take reservations. There were six people in his group. I called the restaurant, explained that I was with the Ritz-Carlton and I knew they didn't take reservations. I asked if they could put this group on the waiting list now so they wouldn't have a long wait when they got there. The manager agreed to make an exception and hold a table for our guest. I told her that she should contact me if she ever needed anything from the Ritz-Carlton, because I wanted to return the favor that she was doing for me. After our guest and his party left, the doorman told me that this guest worked directly for the hotel's owner. I didn't realize who he was and that the hotel's owner was in his group. It's a good thing that I treat everybody like they're important."

Shift Work

The hotel is open 24 hours a day, but the concierge staff works different shifts from 6:30 a.m. until 11:00 p.m. During her five-day workweek, Lynn ideally works two morning shifts (6:30 to 3), a mid-day shift (11 a.m. to 7:30 p.m.), and one or two evening shifts (2:30 to 11). "When my kids aren't with me, I like to work the evening shift. I can be a 'Mommy helper' at school and have lunch with my kids."

CAREER CHECKLIST

You'll like this job if you …

- Are friendly and open to people

- Are not judgmental

- Are tuned into people's needs

- Like to help people

- Go above and beyond in effort to solve problems

- Pay attention to detail

(Lynn is divorced. She and her ex-husband share custody of their four children. She has a live-in person to help her at home.) "When I have my kids, I try to work the morning shift so I'm home when school is out."

Before her shift starts, Lynn changes into her uniform. "Then I go to line-up. Each department has a line-up for every shift. Everyone working in the hotel must attend

A Take-Charge Person

Lynn grew up in Norfolk, Virginia, and has two younger brothers. Her father is an optometrist. She had a stay-at-home mom. Lynn belonged to many groups in school, but "my favorite thing was being a Girl Scout."

Lynn's mother died when she was 15 years old. "I became a mother fig-

When I have a very demanding guest, I pretend that

he is a secret shopper so I won't lose my composure.

line-up to learn what's happening during that shift. We learn who the manager on duty is; the number of guests in the hotel; how many guests are arriving and departing; the VIP (Very Important Person) guests; what conventions or events like a wedding are going on; and what guests have had a problem. When a guest has a problem, we not only want to solve it, we want to make sure she doesn't have another problem."

ure for my brothers." Lynn has always been a take-charge, care-giving person, so she was able to rise to this challenge.

Lynn was good in math and science and thought about being a doctor. She attended the University of Miami in Florida. "I wasn't there long when I realized I didn't want to be a doctor. I missed my family."

Lynn returned to Norfolk where Susie Mersel, her mother's friend and Lynn's mentor even today, helped her get a job as assistant to the treasurer of a company that ran several Holiday Inns. Lynn's office was located in their largest hotel. "Even though I didn't work directly for the hotel, I worked in the hotel. I got to interact with the guests, which I enjoyed." Lynn wanted to work directly for the hotel, but they weren't hiring.

She next got a job selling advertising for a radio station, the only woman salesperson, and she made lots of money. When the station was sold, Lynn got a job with a magazine, selling advertising space. Then Lynn met Steven, a lawyer, through their common interest in politics. They married and moved to the Washington, DC, area. Lynn helped Steven in his law practice during their 15-year marriage, while raising 4 children. "I quietly watched the secretary while she was being trained on the computer so I could learn, too." When Steven's father was too ill to do the bookkeeping, Lynn helped him. "I have no accounting degree, but I love math, so I learned about accounting." Lynn eventually took over the ac-

counting functions and managed the law firm from home, so she'd be there for the children.

Good Career Advice

After her divorce, Lynn worked part time for a temporary agency and took courses at Northern Virginia Community College. "The most exciting job I'd ever had was working in the hotel," Lynn told her career advisor, who sug-

gested a course she could take that would help her decide. That course, taught by Howard Reichbart who still mentors her today, convinced her and she signed up for hospitality management. There were subjects that Lynn wasn't interested in, like safety and sanitation, so she didn't enroll in a certification or degree program. "For my 10-year plan, I thought I'd like to be a hotel manager." Lynn took the meeting planner course. (Meeting planners do all the work for organizations that sponsor big conventions at hotels.) "I realized that I wanted to work in a convention hotel, but I did not want to be a meeting planner."

During 2000, Lynn accepted a job at the concierge desk of the Hyatt Regency Crystal City in Arlington, Virginia. "I knew that this was where I wanted to be." The Hyatt's head concierge was also the president of the Washington (DC) Area Concierge Association. "I knew I could learn a lot from her."

After six months at the concierge desk, the hotel's general manager asked Lynn what department she wanted to transfer to. He was making

her a supervisor, since she had told him she wanted to be a hotel manager. Lynn chose a meeting concierge position (the hotel representative who works with

stay in Washington hotels. Lynn was working fewer hours and making less money. "But in early 2002, the Ritz-Carlton, where I'd always wanted to

Each department has a line-up for every shift. Everyone working in the hotel must attend line-up to learn what's happening during that shift.

meeting planners). "I didn't do any planning. I just executed others' plans. When groups arrived, it was challenging. After they were settled, it was boring. I dreaded going to work." This job made Lynn rethink her career goal. "I realized that I didn't want management, I wanted to be a concierge."

However, the general manager wouldn't approve her transfer back to the concierge desk. Knowing she was unhappy about that, a fellow concierge working at the Omni Shoreham in downtown Washington told her about a concierge job opening at this hotel. "He told me the job was mine. It was a perfect fit."

After the September 11, 2001, terrorist attack, few people traveled to

work, posted a concierge job." She applied. "I researched the Washington Ritz-Carlton through the Internet and newspaper articles to learn everything I could. The interview process was tough. I went there six times. They wanted a concierge who had keys. This means that the concierge belongs to an organization called Les Clefs d'Or, which is French for 'the keys of gold.' A concierge must meet many stringent requirements to get their keys. Now, becoming a member and getting keys is my goal." Even though Lynn didn't have keys, she got the job and started working February 2002 at the Ritz-Carlton, where she is the only female concierge.

Kathryn Kincannon

Kathryn Kincannon

Managing Director, Lake Placid Lodge, Lake Placid, NY

Major, Psychology

Hotel General Manager

Behind the Scenes at a Four-Star Resort

Kathryn was giddy from lack of sleep when the phone rang at the Carter House Victorians in Eureka, California, in late July 1994. Up since 3:00 a.m. organizing an on-site breakfast for the film crew of the movie *Outbreak* (who had set up headquarters at the small inn she was temporarily managing), the farthest thing from Kathryn's mind was a new job. When she heard David Garrett ask if she might be interested in running a hotel he was building in the Adirondack ski resort of Lake Placid in upstate New York, she blithely quipped, "The Adirondacks … isn't that where they filmed the movie *Deliverance*? "No," David laughed, "that was Appalachia." And even though Lake Placid had hosted two Olympic games, in her mind, East Coast mountains were

General Manager

To become general manager of a hotel, you have to pay your dues by working up through the ranks. This means starting as an employee for low hourly pay, then working for promotions to supervisor and department head.

The average salary for a general manager at a small hotel (less than 100 rooms) is $100,000 to $150,000 a year plus benefits; for a large hotel, $500,000 a year.

KATHRYN'S CAREER PATH

Loves being
▼ outdoors,
likes tennis

Graduates
▼ college, moves
to mountains

Works as
▼ waitress/realtor,
marries/divorces

mole hills compared to the majestic peaks of the west and Europe. Besides, Kathryn had vowed to work only for herself after leaving her last job of managing a small upscale hotel near Yosemite National Park—to never work "for" someone again.

"But I was really exhausted," Kathryn remembers of David's offer to fly her to look at his new hotel. "The wild work schedule of this movie-making was nuts, so I said yes, just out of curiosity, and to sleep a couple of days and regroup." Eight years later, she's still in Lake Placid, the managing director of Lake Placid Lodge, and loving every minute of it.

Hospitality Philosophy

Kathryn took the helm of the Lake Placid Lodge two weeks after it opened, in August of 1994. "It was a nightmare," she remembers, "full of untrained staff and guests arriving for rooms that had not even been built yet! But the setting of ancient mountains, majestic pines, and tranquil waters was pure magic. I intuitively knew it would never go out of style. Best of all, the Garretts and I

Works in Palm
▼ Springs, returns
to mountains

Writes
▼ prospectuses and
travel book, travels

Runs restaurants,
▼ manages hotel in
Yosemite

truly connected as people—personally and professionally. They renewed my faith in the power of working as a team to accomplish grand results."

But success didn't come right away. "The biggest challenge I faced upon opening the Lodge was an identity crisis—the property looked and felt like a romantic hideaway, but it was being promoted as a family destination."

The Garretts' other Adirondack property, The Point, catered to couples only, so they decided the Lodge property would be for families. "But the way guests would exhale when they sat in big chairs on the lakefront at sunset with the loon calls ringing through the mist, I was certain the Lodge's spirit was peaceful serenity, not a high-energy family playground." Many philosophical discussions ensued over the next couple of years be-

tween Kathryn and the Garretts, until she finally convinced them the Lodge's highest and best use was catering to couples who needed a reprieve from the stresses of their daily lives, including their children.

Today, the Lake Placid Lodge is a member of the prestigious Relais & Chateaux hotel association, a Mobil 4-star since 1997, and ranked in the Top 20 Small Hotels and Resorts in the country by the Zagat Survey. "We get tremendous press from every magazine imaginable, and the number of repeat guests is growing by leaps and bounds. Yet, there's never a day I feel like it's done. Success is in the details. And I'm constantly striving to make improvements and implement new ideas to make this unique Adirondack experience even more memorable from a guest perspective."

77

KATHRYN'S CAREER PATH

Starts marketing
▼ company for small
hotels

Visits Lake
▼ Placid Lodge,
becomes manager

Working in Paradise

Kathryn works five to six days a week, usually starting around 9:00 a.m. "Sometimes I arrive early, just for the surprise factor." Her day doesn't end until 8:00 p.m. or later. "Last night I got called at 1:00 a.m. about a chimney fire. It's just the nature of this business to expect the unexpected."

"The hotel business, by its very nature, is like a family—we work so closely together in such an intense environment that we all 'know' each other inside and out. We also know that 'family' can bring out both the best and worst in us. I have over 100 people working for me at any one time—if people aren't respectful of each other it affects their work."

Kathryn thus spends the first couple of hours of her day "reading the pulse of my guests and my staff." She first goes down to the dining room during breakfast and chats with guests—gauging the temperature of their happiness. When the guests all seem content, she'll wander through the different departments—restaurant, housekeeping, grounds, front desk—chatting with her managers (of whom eight report directly to her) and her assistant manager to see how the day is shaping up. "I make sure there isn't anything gnawing at them that will prevent them from total enthusiasm for their work that day."

Kathryn sees the hotel business as a stage performance. "We all have a role to play. If there are players who aren't emotionally 'up' for their role, the whole system can break down, which is completely unacceptable. It's my job to motivate and inspire my team to be the best they can be and work well together. If I do that, I've succeeded. If I don't, I've failed. It's really that simple."

The middle part of Kathryn's day involves office work. She writes welcome letters for every guest, noting specifics like anniversaries, birthdays, repeat stays, honeymoons, etc. "I may not have time to meet and greet each guest, but through my welcome letter, they get a sense of who I am and what the property stands for. It assures them we pay attention to details—and we do so from the top down." Kathryn then takes care of emails and phone messages, works on financial reports, and other correspondence.

After a couple of hours, it's time to get out of the office and get moving— she's not one to stay still for too long. She'll go take a walk around the property, checking guest rooms. "Every time my staff see me coming, they know I'll find something that needs attention—a closet to clean, an un-ironed uniform, geraniums that need dead-heading, a window that needs washing. It may irritate them in the moment, but they respect the fact that

CAREER CHECKLIST ✓

You'll like this
   job if you ...

Are curious, like to explore

Can change, are not set in your ways

Are open to new adventures, will try new things

Are flexible, can adapt to different styles

Have a sense of humor

Are interested in people and can 'read' people

Will pay attention to details, and can handle many different tasks

I don't let anything slide." Kathryn meets weekly with each of her department heads for a half hour, one-on-one session, and they all gather as a group every Thursday.

On occasion, somewhere during her day, Kathryn will give a T'ai Chi (a Chinese exercise and meditation) lesson to a house guest. "I let guests know I'm available for a complimentary lesson if they would like one. A surprising number actually take me up on it. It gives me a couple hours to go do something I love in one of the most beautiful settings on earth."

Then, when all's quiet on the hotel front, usually not until 7:00 or 8:00 p.m., Kathryn will finish up whatever office work is needed to clear her desk. She then writes a "To Do" list for the following day, puts a leash on her dog Sachi (a six-year-old Akita that comes to work with her every day), and heads home to "Rainbow's End," her lakefront sanctuary about a 30-minute drive from the Lodge. "The drive gives me time to download and release the day fully before I get home. Once there, my ritual is to have a Zen moment or two—soak in my outdoor hot tub, let the wind blow the cares of the day away, and bask in the beauty of pure solitude. There are only two other full-time residents on the lake I live on, so it's blissfully quiet all year round."

From Ski Bum to Hotel Manager

Kathryn grew up in a Los Angeles, California, suburb. "My parents, in effect, raised two families. They had my older brother when they were quite young. Twenty-two years later, with my brother in medical school, they had their second child, my older sister, followed by my brother and I (twins), followed by my younger sister two years after that. When my dad died two years ago, my parents had been married for 64 years. My mom's still going strong, sharp as a tack at age 85. They were truly an amazing couple—a fact I'm only now fully appreciating."

Kathryn's mother was a high school teacher, her father an accountant. They had very high expectations for their children, including receiving a college education. "We never missed school. We were expected to be the best at everything we did—be it academics or playing softball. It was an unspoken rule in our house, and everyone lived up to it."

Kathryn, as did her siblings, graduated from Stanford University with honors. Although her degree was in

kicked into gear. "I was determined to become street-wise and people-savvy. But I was so young and naïve—I had been sheltered all my life. To finally be in the 'real world' was exhilarating at first. Until I found out what it felt like to rack up credit card debt without the money to pay it back. Until I got fired

> **I always strove to be the best at whatever I did, and I believed that if I made decisions with my heart and soul they would take me down the right path.**

Psychology, with a minor in Philosophy, she "had no idea what I wanted to do with my life—no direction, no ambition. I was a bit of a free spirit. So I decided on a whim to move to Mammoth Lakes, a beautiful ski resort in the Sierra Nevadas. My father hit the roof and disowned me. He had it all planned that I would go to work for some Fortune 500 company in some management trainee position, but that just wasn't me. I didn't know what I wanted, but I knew it wasn't that. So I rebelled and struck out on my own."

That's when Kathryn's life-lessons

from my first job for not bothering to show up on time. Until I had my heart broken by the first love of my life."

"I found out I was a survivor—that I was tough and never let anything get me down for long. I started to believe in myself, learned how to roll with the punches, and realized that no matter what I was going through, tomorrow would be a better day. It always was."

During these formative years, Kathryn's only motivator was a passion for living well and a strong desire to see and experience as much of the world as possible. She felt that if she lived in places that nurtured her need for peace and beauty—be that a roaring ocean or an ancient wilderness—where she could indulge her love of nature via skiing, horseback riding, T'ai Chi, playing tennis, hiking and sailing, piano and poetry, she would find a career to suit her. She moved ten times in ten years to drop-dead gorgeous mountain resorts that tickled her fancy—Lake Tahoe; Jackson Hole, Wyoming; Yosemite National Park; the Rockies; Oregon Cascades; the Alps; and finally, Lake Placid—and had just as many jobs, from waiting tables to selling real estate, managing restaurants to travel writing, or working in various capacities in the hotel industry.

"I've done so many 'jobs' in my life—whatever I felt was challenging and interesting at the time—and I never worried about where it would take me or what it would bode for the future. I always strove to be the best at whatever I did, and I believed that if I made decisions with my heart and soul they would take me down the right path."

Her Resume Sums It Up

Strangely enough, that's exactly how Kathryn ended up managing the Lake Placid Lodge. "A friend in the hotel business asked me about 10 years ago for my resume. (He knew it was time I moved on from the hotel I was managing at the time, that I had a hard time letting go because I had been so involved in it for so long—from concept to raising the money, to getting it built, to actually running it.) I had never written a resume throughout my entire career, and when I finally did, I was amazed at how well my progression looked on paper."

It was that resume that made David Garrett so certain Kathryn was the absolutely perfect person to run his new hotel in the Adirondacks. The diversity of her experience in the variety of locations gave her depth and seasoned hospitality sense. Her love of resorts told him that she could survive, even savor, the seasonality of the resort side of the business. Her wanderlust and wide range of hobbies and recreational pursuits told him she was an interesting person who could hold her own with sophisticated travelers. What seemed scattered in the making proved the ideal recipe for career success.

Which just makes Kathryn shake her head and smile at the serendipity of it all. "When I see how destiny has played a role in my life, I am all the more grateful that I focused on how I lived rather than what I did to make a living."

But that doesn't mean Kathryn is content and ready to settle down into happily-ever-after. "Far from it!" she laughs. "I'm wise enough to know that what makes me happy and fulfilled tomorrow may be totally different than today. When I feel the timing is right to make a change, I'll do it with an open mind and a willing heart, embrace it fully, and hold on for the ride!"

"Change is the only constant in my life—and I find it fascinating. It provides such an opportunity for growth and learning new things. I make a conscious effort to learn something new every year—be that scuba diving or jumping a horse—and to travel to a totally unfamiliar culture and immerse myself in the

way other people live and think. Living life to the fullest is my idea of a noble endeavor. And I intend to do just that."

Marg Dente & Gail Kinney

Marg Dente & Gail Kinney

Innkeepers / Owners, Owl's Nest Inn at Engadine, Candler, NC

Marg, major in Creative Arts; Gail, Computer Science

Innkeepers, Bed and Breakfast

Their Home is Your Home

Innkeeper Marg Dente and her long-time friend and fellow innkeeper Gail Kinney both love to cook, "especially breakfast. The challenge is to come up with a different breakfast each day for guests who stay more than one week. We each have specialty dishes, and so far, we've been able to meet that challenge."

When guests check in at the Owl's Nest Inn, a bed and breakfast (B&B) in the mountains of North Carolina, Marg tells them, "Coffee is at 8 a.m.; breakfast is at 9; breakfast is soggy by 9:15; and at 9:30 I eat it." (B&Bs are usually large old homes, having four or more bedrooms and baths, where guests can enjoy the living room, porches, and other common rooms. The innkeepers also live in the house

Innkeepers

People who start their own business may not earn any salary in the beginning. They invest their own money in the business, and they get more money through loans or venture capital. Until they make a profit or "go public" by selling stock, they probably pay themselves a small salary and put profits back into the business to help it grow. They also plan to make money when they sell the business.

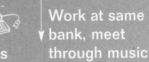
or on the grounds and prepare a special breakfast for the guests. Inns are usually larger, often serve all meals, but also have home-like areas where guests can spend time.)

A Time for Change

During the late 1990s, Marg saw an ad in the Sunday newspaper for a seminar about becoming an innkeeper. She talked Gail into going with her. Both women had been working at Duke Power in Charlotte, North Carolina, for 18 years. Marg was a nuclear technician who had finally made supervisor. However, with the promotion came responsibility for laying people off. Gail was a computer specialist in the information technology department. "Corporations did not value employees like

they used to, so we were ready for a change. Being able to run our own business and make our own decisions was appealing."

Gail and Marg knew that they wanted to move to Asheville, North Carolina, a tourist destination in the Great Smoky Mountains. They followed the seminar with a three-day workshop on innkeeping. "After that, we were hooked. We consulted the workshop provider, David Caples of Lodging Resources, to learn how much money we would need to become innkeepers and when we could to do it." In 1997, they took their savings and bought the Owl's Nest Inn, which is 15 minutes from downtown Asheville. "We beat his time frame by two years."

Leave bank for jobs
▼ with Duke Power

Attend workshop on
▼ innkeeping

Leave Duke
▼ Power, move to
Asheville

Teamwork Grows the Business

Business for everyone in the travel and tourism industry slowed considerably after the September 11, 2001, terrorist attacks. "Our occupancy rate was soaring that year. It was higher than occupancy at the inns downtown." The Owl's Nest got a lot of guests in October, when the leaves are so colorful. "A lot of people canceled their long-distance trips and visited places closer to home." Unfortunately, business slowed after that, but Marg and Gail work as a team to attract guests and keep their inn going.

While Gail worked at Duke Power, she dealt with Serena Software, a company in California that sold its products to Duke. Anticipating the move to Asheville, Gail approached the company for a job. They hired her full-time to help their various customers, which she does as a telecommuter—using her computer at home to communicate with customers all over the states. Gail contributes income from her job to help pay for the inn's operating costs. On weekends she helps Marg, who manages the inn full time. Gail does the accounting and paperwork for the inn. Marg does the selling and marketing.

When it comes to promoting the B&B, Marg learned a lot by being active in the Asheville Bed and Breakfast Association. "At first, I thought we should market our B&B like the downtown inns do, but we took a different approach because we are out in the country." An example is what they did for the New Year's Eve millennium celebration.

Gail takes telecommuting
job with Serena Software

Buy Owl's Nest,
become innkeepers

For the three nights of the 2000 millennium celebration, Marg and Gail developed several New Year's Eve guest packages. They included the usual room and breakfast for two along with champagne and appetizers

were concerned they wouldn't fill their rooms. We filled our rooms early because our rates were so reasonable." The downtown innkeepers had arranged for only one bus to transport their guests. "Our guests had a limou-

This is everybody's dream job, but don't do it if you're expecting to make lots of money.

at the inn. Then the guests would ride in a limousine (which was reserved back in July) to a downtown special dinner arranged by all the inns participating in the New Year's celebration. "We divided the costs and built in a small profit. Many other inns, wanting a large profit from each package, set their package rates so high that, the week before the celebration, they

sine at their disposal and could leave whenever they wished."

When tourism is down during the winter, Marg promotes the inn with murder mystery weekends. "A woman in Colorado writes the mysteries. While other inns aren't doing much business, these mystery weekends fill our rooms and get us through those slow months." Murder mystery guests arrive Friday evening and leave Sunday morning. "It's hectic on Friday when we must check them in and prepare and serve hors d'oeuvres to start the weekend. On Saturday we give out clues. If guests go to a restaurant on Saturday evening, I contact the restaurant and arrange for their food server to give our guests a clue while they're at dinner, which really surprises them. We give a prize to the guests who solve the mystery."

Running the Inn

Gail and Marg do much of the inn's routine maintenance themselves, but "we're not handymen. We probably hire for a lot of work that a man-and-woman partnership could do themselves." Like many homeowners, they hire experts for big jobs. "We hired a landscaper. We have someone do the yard work. We hire an electrician when needed, because as a business we must have a permit and the work must pass inspection. It's most important to find someone reliable, who won't overcharge. We have a

CAREER CHECKLIST ✓

You'll like this job if you ...

- Are outgoing
- Like to take care of people
- Like to entertain people
- Can learn how to fix things
- Like to prepare and serve food
- Can manage money
- Like old homes, decorating

wonderful relationship with a handyman here."

Karen Miller is their inn assistant. She helps with the day-to-day work, such as cleaning the rooms and doing laundry. "When we have guests, we have to be pleasant and on our toes all the time. There are days when we're on our feet from 7 a.m. to 11 p.m., but we're doing it for ourselves."

A typical work cycle begins when Marg checks in the guests between 3 and 6 p.m. Then Marg and Gail serve light snacks and drinks in the living room during social hour from 5 to 6 p.m. "Because we serve wine during social hour, we card anyone who looks under 21." After the guests leave for dinner, Marg and Gail retire to the back of the inn where they live, but not before setting the table and preparing some of the food for the next morning's breakfast.

The next morning, Gail is up first, so she makes coffee. "If we're serving a casserole, I put it in the oven." Marg is in the kitchen by 8:30. Breakfast is served at 9, with music. After breakfast, they clear the table and leave the guests alone to chat. Gail does dishes while Marg prepares the bills for guests checking out. They both prepare picnic baskets for guests who request them. They provide guests with directions and maps to where they want to go—trails, waterfalls, antique shops, restaurants—and make dinner reservations. By this time it's noon, and Karen has started cleaning; everyone helps with laundry. People call to get information, so the phone rings all day. The best time for Marg and Gail to run errands—such as groceries, banking, dry cleaning—is between check-out (11 a.m.) and check-in (3 p.m.). The most difficult

> There are days when we're on our feet from 7 a.m. to 11 p.m., but we're doing it for ourselves.

time for Marg is when Gail is traveling and Karen is not there. "I must do it all myself."

During the day, the women handle other tasks—preparing confirmation letters and sending out information about weddings and other events. In North Carolina, innkeepers must live on the property. "In this business, you must make an effort to have your own time. Some guests will try to see us after 11 p.m. if we let them. We provide them with an emergency telephone number which rings in our rooms." (Marg is trained in first aid and cardiopulmonary resuscitation.)

Marg and Gail think that two women running an inn is an asset. "The guests like to talk about how we got into it. The men are curious. For many women, owning an inn is a dream, so they're really interested."

The Road to Owl's Nest

Marg was born in Chicago, Illinois, and raised in Charlotte. She was good in math and loved music as a child. Although she thought about being a veterinarian, she pursued music; she plays classical guitar. After graduating high school, she enrolled in Brevard College in western North Carolina where she got a two-year degree in music. She transferred to East Carolina University where she changed her major to music therapy. She then transferred to the University of North Carolina, Charlotte, where she graduated with a degree in creative arts.

Gail was born and raised in Charlotte. She took college prep courses and accounting in high school and started to study accounting in college. However, Gail had health problems and her mother died when she was 19. She quit college and got a job with A&P grocery stores, where she worked her way up to head bookkeeper. Then Gail married and moved to Virginia. Three years later, after her divorce, she moved back to Charlotte and went back to school. At 26,

she enrolled in Central Piedmont Community College in Charlotte where she got a technical degree in computer science.

Gail worked in the check-processing department at a bank while attending college. In 1973, Marg was working at the same bank to support herself while she pursued a career in music. Gail, who was a singer, and Marg were asked to help with the music for a Christmas show the bank's employees were producing. They met through music and have been friends ever since.

Marg left the bank first. "I was training young men, recent college graduates, to do my job so they could become branch managers and go straight to the top. Fed up one day, I walked across the street and applied for a job at Duke Power. I did well on the test; my math really came in handy. I got a nuclear technician position. I worked there 18 years, reaching my goal of becoming a supervisor."

When she tired of the shift work for her job at the bank, Gail applied at Duke Power and got a job in their investor relations department. She later transferred to the information technology department.

The Future

After getting settled at Owl's Nest, Marg and Gail wanted to purchase the land behind their inn for future expansion. "The property was special to the woman who owned it. The previous owner of Owl's Nest wasn't able to negotiate a deal with her. I think that, being women, we understood the owner's attachment to the property. We worked with her and negotiated a deal to buy the property." They plan to build guest cabins on the property, which will fill fast when the nearby golf course is completed.

Running the inn allows little time for hobbies, but Gail and Marg like to travel. They go to Key West for one week every January and spend time over the July 4 holiday in Tennessee. To furnish the inn, they have become collectors, so they enjoy going to yard sales and antique shows.

Ellen McGinnis

Ellen McGinnis

Spa Director, The Grove Park Inn Resort & Spa, Asheville, NC

Major, Early Childhood Education

Spa Director

It's All About Relaxation, Renewal, and Creating Memories

After graduating high school, Ellen McGinnis didn't want to go to college. "I wanted to move from Florida to North Carolina to be a mountain woman. My parents had other ideas. They had submitted an application to Saint Mary's College, Notre Dame, Indiana. I was accepted, so I went there."

Although her life took many turns, today Ellen lives in North Carolina's Blue Ridge Mountains. She is the Spa Director at the Grove Park Inn Resort & Spa in Asheville. The 510-room Grove Park Inn, built in 1913 from granite boulders from the mountains, is a member of Historic Hotels of America. *USA Today* has rated its 40,000-square-foot spa as one of the world's top 10.

Spa Consultant
Consultants make a percentage of the project. Possibility is between $45,000 and $350,000 a year.

Spa Director
Depends upon size and location of spa. Base salaries range from $55,000 to $200,000. A bonus is standard and determined on a monthly percentage or a yearly performance.

From Ocean to Mountains

Before arriving at the Grove Park Inn, Ellen worked for WTS, an international consulting firm for creating and managing resort spas. "As a consultant, I was in the center of the construction, opening, and first-year-of-business phases for spas. It was insane, but I loved it. In this business there aren't many construction companies experienced in building spas. For example, I know we don't want wood molding or a wood door in a steam room. Architects don't know the many functions and the workflow for designing spas, like the best place to locate the dirty linen. I've learned about spa construction and design from my work experience. After doing it so many times, I know what not to do."

Ellen knows about buying equipment and products for a spa. "You form relationships with the vendors. You learn how to shop."

Ellen knows how to market a spa. "These resorts wanted spas, but they didn't understand the spa business, like what types of treatments—facials, body scrubs, massages—could be offered to guests. We also wrote the job descriptions and standard operating procedures for running the spa because no one else knew the specifics."

When Ellen learned about the Grove Park's planned spa, she and her three children—Sara, Kaylen, and John—were living on the Outer Banks (barrier islands) of North Carolina, where Ellen was managing a project for WTS. "It was a showcase property. The company flew clients there to show them what we could cre-

ate for their property. I assisted in the sale of a management package."

Within two years, Ellen's job for this project would end. "Then I would have to go to the corporate office in Washington, DC, which I didn't want to do. I wanted my children to live where they would be nurtured and where we would have balance between work and leisure in our lives." When Ellen interviewed for Spa Director at the Grove Park Inn, Craig Madison, the Grove Park's general manager, told her about their work culture. "He added, 'I want you to come here because you want to settle here with your family.' I realized I needed to do this."

Building a World-Class Spa

Ellen arrived at the Grove Park Inn one year before the spa opened. She played a key role in its construction. She says that the Grove Park's culture is supportive of her as a woman. "In my past, men challenged my ability when it came to construction. I've worked with all men on the Grove Park's spa project and they've always shown me respect."

Ellen hired more than 100 employees. "Our hiring process is intensive. The therapists must be nationally and state certified before being interviewed. We profile them and do six in-

I ate, drank, and slept the fitness industry. I enjoyed

learning everything about the business.

ELLEN'S CAREER PATH

terviews. Then we do a practical—they give a treatment to me or the 'back-of-the-house' manager (who supervises the treatment staff such as massage therapists and nail technicians). Within their first 12 months of working here, the therapists must commit to getting 5 advanced certifications." Ellen developed training programs. She teaches new employees a basic course and does much of the training for aestheticians (skin care specialists) herself. "We teach the therapists everything from how to greet a guest through how to send them off when their treatment is completed." Staff development is very important to Ellen. "I want my assistants to know as much about the business as I do."

Ellen decided upon all of the spa's treatments and equipment. "We've been very successful. We turned a profit our fifth month. We didn't expect to do that until our third year."

On the Job 24/7

Ellen's job is a three-minute walk from her home. Part of her job is to look the part, to look like she gets regular spa treatments—manicures, facials, massages. "I don't get a treatment often, but sometimes the staff arrange one for me. They take care of me. Being a spa director is very demanding and difficult. Many people leave after three years." Ellen says the key is to have a good, supportive staff.

Ellen is on call 24 hours a day. Her days can start at 7:30 a.m. "Sometimes I'm here 12 to 14 hours, sometimes 8." She first checks everything.

"The shift supervisor arrives at 6:30 a.m. and does a walk-through." Ellen checks with the 'front-of-the-house' manager (who oversees administration, the concierge, the gift and snack shops, and maintenance). "As director, I develop a vision for them and assign projects with goals. I lead the troops to the vision. I rarely collect data or do spreadsheets myself." Ellen established the operating standards and systems. "Nobody has to reinvent the wheel. They just have to do their job."

Ellen gets daily updates. "I need financial and other data to know where we are in relation to our plan. I review complaint logs and managers' logs. If an employee or a family member is ill, I want to know how she's doing."

Like most hotel divisions, spa employees must attend a pre-shift meeting, called a line-up, everyday to learn what's happening. "I review the day's activity sheet every morning so I know what's going on, like whether media will be here and who the VIP (very important person) guests are. I like to attend line-up four times a

CAREER CHECKLIST ✓

You'll like this
job if you …

Like to be in charge, take responsibility

Like to keep learning

Like challenges, can handle many different tasks

Aren't afraid to try new things

Don't expect to start at the top

Can make a commitment

Care about people

week to say hello and give my staff awards. Housekeeping and maintenance get done after we close for business."

Like all high-level managers, Ellen must attend meetings everyday. She is a member of the Grove Park's senior leadership team. "We make decisions that affect the whole hotel."

Ellen spends an hour each day on 'floor time' when she goes to the treatment area to get feedback from the guests. "It's nice to hear someone say 'I haven't relaxed this much in years.' The job sometimes desensitizes one to the beauty of everything. Client feedback is my reward for the hard work."

Ellen is working on a new brochure for new treatments. "I want to use more stones, water, and mountain herbs. Branding—having treatments unique to the Grove Park Spa that will identify us in the market—is important. I never want a guest to say 'I got a massage like that at home.' We want to create a memory." Ellen's not afraid to try new things, but she tracks their cost and the feedback.

A Beach Ballerina

Ellen grew up in Sarasota, Florida, with her older brother, Steve, and her younger sister, Carole. "We were beach kids." Her mother was an editor with the *Miami Herald*. Her father was a reconstructive surgeon who specialized in helping burn victims. "He was also a sculptor."

Ellen loved ballet. Her grandmother and great-grandmother were prima ballerinas. When her school day ended, she attended a school for the performing arts. "Theater and dance were my loves."

During her senior year in high school, Ellen suffered a broken foot. That ended her dream of being a dancer. "I had a great experience at Saint Mary's college, but I transferred to Florida State in Tallahassee because of their dance program, even though I couldn't have a dance career." Ellen majored in early childhood education with minors in social work and dance.

Finds Her Calling

At the beginning of her junior year, Ellen's father gave her enough money for the whole college quarter. "I spent it in three weeks, so I had to get a job." Ellen's roommate arranged for Ellen to take over her job in a figure salon. "I was a senior service consultant. This was in the mid-1970s. They used old-fashioned equipment to jiggle you or press you to get the weight off. We've come a long way from that, but that's where I found my calling. I realized I could make money and make people feel good."

Six weeks after graduation, Ellen married her college sweetheart. "My father had retired and bought the Piedmont Inn in Haywood County, North Carolina, so we got married on top of a mountain near Asheville."

Ellen was living in Venice, Florida, when she took her first aerobics class after her first child, Sara, was born. She loved it but knew she could do better, so she opened her own aerobics studio. "I devoured the business. I went to as many workshops as I could,

talked with fitness specialists. I got up at 6 a.m. to watch exercise shows. I read books and took five classes a day. I entered competitions." Ellen also found that she loved hospitality when she helped at her parents' inn. She was able to combine those loves as the fitness director at Colony Beach & Tennis Resort on Longboat Key, Florida. "That's how I got my start in resorts. I learned about marketing, sales, and statistical analysis."

Life-Defining Situations

Five days after Ellen had her second child, Kaylen, the family moved to Orlando, Florida. "My father-in-law had a heart attack. My husband took over his business." Ellen became a training supervisor for a fitness company. Later, when she was told to train a new male employee, a recent college graduate, who would then become her boss, she told the director that she wanted the management job. "He told me I couldn't because I was a wife and mother." Ellen quit. Her next job was as a sales manager.

"The man I worked for was very supportive." She continued her aerobics and even participated locally in aerobics competitions and went to regionals when she was six months pregnant with her third child. "My boss told me to take off as much time as I needed for the baby."

When John was four months old, Ellen's husband left her and their children. She went back to work to learn that her boss was closing the business because his wife was ill. Ellen interviewed for a job to sell advertising for direct mail. "This woman told me that she never hired single mothers, but she said she liked my spunk, so she hired me."

Spa Business

One day Ellen's sister Carole called to encourage Ellen to answer a want ad for a fitness director. "She said they wanted a handwritten application. I was home with the flu, so I prepared an eight-page handwritten application. When they called for an interview, the man said he wanted to meet the woman who submitted a handwritten application. During the interview I learned the owner's wife was in my aerobics class. At the end of the interview, they asked me how much salary I wanted." The job was with International Management Group (IMG) at Isleworth, a community owned by golfer Arnold Palmer where celebrities lived. "They had a clubhouse with a spa and a fitness and recreation program. I was director of eight different activities."

While working at Isleworth, Ellen was a construction consultant for another Palmer spa project at Bay Hill Club & Lodge. "I had gone through four phases of construction at Isleworth, so I had lots of experience." They hired her from Isleworth. Ellen worked for Bay Hill until she was recruited by WTS.

Ellen vacations by visiting family in Florida. She helps her community by serving food at a homeless shelter and helps other single moms. Despite her demanding job, she works at leading a balanced life. "Most of my free time gets lost in decorating. Cooking is my newest passion." She loves the outdoors and likes to hike. She still practices ballet, privately. "But being with my kids is the greatest."

Getting Started On Your
Own Career Path

Getting Started On

Your Own Career Path

WHAT TO DO NOW

To help you prepare for a career in the travel and hospitality fields, the women interviewed for this book recommend things you can do now, while still in school.

TRAVEL

CRUISE SHIP SOCIAL HOSTESS — AMANDA REID

Any job on a cruise ship is an excellent way to travel and see the world for any young person who is keen on a career in the travel industry.

INTERPRETIVE GUIDE — ELIZABETH DOMINGUE

Spend lots of time outside. Follow your heart, study what you are interested in, what you love. Don't let people sway you from your path and your passion.

Get as much knowledge as you can about wildlife and plants. Read about them, but also try to get involved with organizations like the Sierra Club, Nature Conservancy, and the Audubon Society so you can be with and learn from people who know about these topics. Study sciences like wildlife, geology, astronomy, and ecology, and learn about cultural history. You need good communication skills to share your knowledge with people. Physical fitness is good for you regardless of what you do in life, but it is especially important for this work.

PHOTOGRAPHER — CATHERINE KARNOW

Have fun and take lots of pictures. To learn the basics, get yourself a decent camera that doesn't have everything automatic but has manual settings. You need to control the *f* stop and the shutter speed. You need to understand focus, depth of field, and ASA film speeds.

Look at photography books in the library, and look at magazines. Many have gorgeous photography. See what interests you. Think seriously about photography as a good career and educate yourself. Read about famous photographers' lives and their works.

TRAVEL AGENT — DONNA CLUCKY

Learn as much as you can about the places you visit. Read about them. Study geography and social studies. Learn as many computer programs as you can. Get a degree in travel. You must know and understand a place to be confident about selling it, so travel as much as you can.

TRAVEL WRITER AND EDITOR — KAREN CURE

Develop a nose for news. Read a lot to learn lots of facts. Write a lot; keep a diary or journal. Work on publications like a school newspaper or yearbook. Write letters and email. Always check your spelling and grammar. The more you write, the better writer you'll be. These are things you must learn early; you can't catch up if you start later. At 21, it's too late to start learning how to write.

HOSPITALITY

GUEST RANCH PROGRAMS MANAGER — GINIFER MACEAU

You need to know about running a business. Don't ignore the people skills for the horse skills because they are tied together. You need people skills. You can get these skills from all of your jobs. Even if you're a wrangler, you must know how to read people. Love what you're doing.

HOTEL CONCIERGE — LYNN JASON

You need to be able to listen attentively and speak well. Studying a foreign language would be helpful in communicating with both foreign guests and hotel staff who may not know English well, or in working in a hotel in another country.

Have an open mind and try new things, like food or music. Visit museums. Practice helping people by giving directions around your town.

Research what is required for hospitality management courses.

HOTEL GENERAL MANAGER — KATHRYN KINCANNON

Don't think you have to know what you're going to do for the rest of your life. Say yes to opportunities, even if they cause upheaval.

Be humble while you're training. Be patient. If you set goals within a time frame, you'll get frustrated. If a job isn't fun, find another job. Management stops respecting you, because if you're not having fun, your unhappiness shows. Be hard worker. Show that you're willing to work.

INNKEEPERS, BED AND BREAKFAST — MARG DENTE AND GAIL KINNEY

Take hospitality/innkeeping courses. Learn what people like. You must be there for your guests, but don't let them treat you like a servant. Be self-confident.

Seek advice when you need to—real estate, financial, legal—a lot of it's free. If you take a business partner, be sure you know and respect each other. Choose a business partner whose abilities complement yours. Don't go into innkeeping until you are financially able. You need money to get you through slow times.

Don't think about being an innkeeper if you want to make lots of money. You'll realize a return on your investment in your inn when you sell it.

SPA DIRECTOR — ELLEN McGINNIS

You will draw upon any experience or skills you've gotten in life—from school, college, music, dance, sports, jobs, anywhere—in this work, so value all of it.

Do something you are passionate about or it's not worth it. Talk with everyone you know and read everything you can to learn about running a business and about resorts and spas.

Remember that you have to start somewhere; you don't leave school and go straight to management. I've hauled laundry and cleaned toilets when I had to; I still would. There's nothing that's not in my job description. Make a commitment.

RECOMMENDED READING

Magazines and books covering the travel and hospitality fields are varied, plentiful, and too numerous to mention. If you enjoy fiction, you can find stories that take place in a city or country—an easy way to learn about the people, culture, and landscape. Check your library or favorite bookstore. Many of the books listed below are recommended by *Best Books for Young Adult Readers,* edited by Stephen Calvert.

FICTION

The Big Wander, by Will Hobbs. Avon/Camelot, 1994. (Two brothers on a trip before one goes to college.)

Captain Hawaii, by Anthony Dana Arkin. Harper Collins, 1994. (16-year-old solves mystery involving tourist boat, evil hotel owner, and dead scientist.)

Forbidden City: A Tale of Modern China, by William Bell. Bantam, 1990. (17-year-old accompanies his cameraman father on assignment to Beijing, China.)

Gulliver's Travels, by Jonathan Swift. Oxford University Press, 1992. (Gulliver's adventures in strange lands.)

Hideout, by Eve Bunting. Harcourt, 1991. (Running away from home, Andy, 12, finds a key for a plush hotel suite.)

Letters from Rifka, by Karen Hesse. Henry Holt, 1992. (12-year-old Rifka tells of her dangerous journey from Russia to United States in 1919.)

Missing Susan: An Elizabeth MacPherson Mystery, by Sharyn McCrumb. Ballentine, 1991. (A group tour of famous murder sights is led by a guide who has been paid to kill one of them.)

Troubling a Star, by Madeleine L'Engle. Farrar, 1994. (A mystery involving nuclear waste when a 16-year-old travels to Antarctica and meets a Baltic prince.)

NONFICTION

A Pioneer Woman's Memoir, edited by J. E. Greenberg and Helen Carey McKeeven. Franklin Watts, 1995. (Trek by covered wagon to Oregon.)

Careers for Travel Buffs and other Restless Types, by Paul Plawin. McGraw Hill/VGM Careers for You, 1995.

Conducting Tours: A Practical Guide (3d ed.), by Marc Mancini. Delmar Learning, 2000.

Exploring Careers on Cruise Ships, by Don Kennedy. Rosen Publishing Group, 1993.

Fitness: Careers Without College, by Maura Rhodes Curless. Peterson's Guides, 1992.

Focus: Five Women Photographers, by Sylvia Wolf. Albert Whitman, 1994.

How to Get a Job with a Cruise Line, 5th ed., by Mary Fallon Miller. Ticket to Adventure, 2000. (Quoted on many Internet sites.)

Inside Secrets to Finding a Career in Travel, by Karen Rubin. JIST Publishing, 2001.

Jobs for Travel Lovers, by Ron and Caryl Krannich. Impact Publications, 2003.

Market Guide for Young Artists and Photographers, by Kathy Henderson. Shoe Tree, 1990.

Market Guide for Young Writers, by Kathy Henderson. Betterway Pubns., 1996.

Margaret Bourke-White: Photographing the World, by Eleanor H. Ayer. Dillon 1992. (A biography.)

Women of the World: Women Travelers & Explorers, by Rebecca Stefoff. Oxford University Press, 1993.

General References

Encyclopedia of Career and Vocational Guidance. Chicago: J. G. Ferguson, 2000.

Career Information Center (7th ed.). Macmillan, 1999.

Peterson's Scholarships, Grants, and Prizes, 2003. Princeton: Peterson's, 2002. (Website: www.petersons.com)

The Girls' Guide to Life: How to Take Charge of the Issues That Affect You, by Catherine Dee. Boston: Little, Brown, 1997. (Celebrates achievements of girls and women, extensive resources.)

THE INTERNET

There are many websites that will give you up-to-date information about travel and hospitality. Several sites list the many types of jobs that support it. Some sites list current job openings. We list a few of these sites below.

JOB SITES

HTTP://MODENA.INTERGATE.CA/BUSINESS/JOBSHIP/

Recruiting agencies have listed job descriptions and answers to frequently asked questions about life at sea.

WWW.CRUISESERVER.NET/TRAVELPAGE/OTHER/JOBS_OVERVIEW.ASP

Provides tips on how to get a job on a cruise ship from author Mary Fallon Miller (see Nonfiction).

WWW.SHIPJOBS.COM

Gives 'insider' information on jobs and advice on how to apply.

WWW.HCAREERS.COM

Lists jobs in hospitality field, posts resumes.

TRAVEL SITES

WWW.SAVVYTRAVELER.COM

Information on trips, also heard on public radio.

WWW.INTREPIDTRAVELER.COM

Information on trips.

ORGANIZATIONS

There are many special interest organizations and groups that serve those in the travel and hospitality industries. Many have informative websites. Here are a few to get you started. Some offer scholarships and some have educational programs for young people.

PROFESSIONAL ORGANIZATIONS

TRAVEL

ADVENTURE TRAVEL SOCIETY

288 North F St., Salida, CO 81201-2107

(303) 649-9016; website: www.adventuretravel.com

AMERICAN SOCIETY OF TRAVEL AGENTS

(Affiliate International Association of Tour Managers, North American Region)

1101 King St., Ste. 200, Alexandria, VA 22314

(703) 739-2782; website: www.astanet.com

INTERNATIONAL GAY AND LESBIAN TRAVEL ASSOCIATION

52 West Oakland Park Blvd., No. 237, Wilton Manors, FL 33310

(954) 776-2626; website: www.iglta.com

NATIONAL TOUR ASSOCIATION

546 East Main St., Lexington, KY 40508-2300

(859) 226-4444; website: www.ntaonline.com

HOSPITALITY

AFRICAN AMERICAN ASSOCIATION OF INNKEEPERS INTERNATIONAL

(877) 422-5777; websites: africanamericaninns.com and africanamericaninns@yahoo.com

AMERICAN BED & BREAKFAST ASSOCIATION

P.O. 1387, Midlothian, VA 23113-8387

(804) 379-2222; website: www.abba.com

AMERICAN HOTEL FOUNDATION

(Offers scholarship.)

1201 New York Ave. NW, Ste. 600, Washington, DC 20005-3931

(202) 289-3180; website: www.ei-ahma.org/ahf/ahf.htm

AMERICAN HOTEL & LODGING ASSOCIATION

(Offers educational training; affiliate Hospitality Sales & Marketing Association International.)

1201 New York Ave. NW, Ste. 600, Washington, DC 20005-3931

(202) 289-3100; website: www.ahlaonline.org

DUDE RANCH ASSOCIATION

Box 471, Laporte, CO 80535

(970) 223-8440; website: www.duderanch.org

INTERNATIONAL COUNCIL ON HOTEL, RESTAURANT AND INSTITUTIONAL EDUCATION

(Programs and internships.)

3205 Skipwith Road, Richmond, VA 23294-4442

(804) 747-4971; website: www.chrie.org/home.html

Les Clef d'Or USA

24088 N. Bridle Trail Road, Lake Forest, IL 60045

Website: www.lesclefsdorusa.com

National Association of Black Hospitality Professionals

(Placement services and educational programs.)

P.O. Box 8132, Columbus, GA 38908-8132

(334) 2988-4802; e-mail: nabhp@aol.com

National Bed & Breakfast Association

P.O. 332, Norwalk, CT 06852

(203) 847-6196; website: www.nbba.com

National Concierge Association

P.O. Box 2860, Chicago, IL 60690-2860

(763) 59109448 or (612) 317-2932; website: www.conciergeassoc.org

National Restaurant Association Educational Foundation

(Video training programs, career information, scholarships.)

250 S. Wacker Drive, Chicago, IL 60506

(312) 715-1010; website: www.edfound.org

How COOL Are You?!

Cool girls like to DO things, not just sit around like couch potatoes. There are many things you can get involved in now to benefit your future. Some cool girls even know what careers they want (or think they want).

Not sure what you want to do? That's fine, too... the Cool Careers series can help you explore lots of careers with a number of great, easy to use tools! Learn where to go and to whom you should talk about different careers, as well as books to read and videos to see. Then, you're on the road to cool girl success!

Written especially for girls, this new series tells what it's like today for women in all types of jobs with special emphasis on nontraditional careers for women. The upbeat and informative pages provide answers to questions you want answered, such as:

✔ **What jobs do women find meaningful?**
✔ **What do women succeed at today?**
✔ **How did they prepare for these jobs?**
✔ **How did they find their job?**
✔ **What are their lives like?**
✔ **How do I find out more about this type of work?**

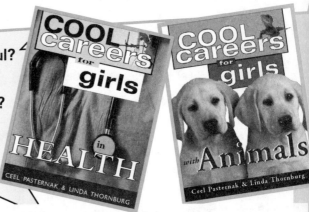

Each book profiles ten women who love their work. These women had dreams, but didn't always know what they wanted to be when they grew up. Zoologist Claudia Luke knew she wanted to work outdoors and that she was interested in animals, but she didn't even know what a zoologist was, much less what they did and how you got to be one. Elizabeth Gruben was going to be a lawyer until she discovered the world of Silicon Valley computers and started her own multimedia company. Mary Beth Quinn grew up in Stowe, Vermont, where she skied competitively and taught skiing. Now she runs a ski school at a Virginia ski resort. These three women's stories appear with others in a new series of career books for young readers.

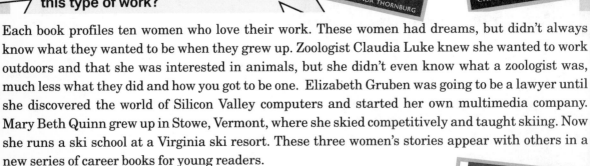

The Cool Careers for Girls series encourages career exploration and broadens girls' career horizons. It shows girls what it takes to succeed, by providing easy-to-read information about careers that young girls may not have considered because they didn't know about them. They learn from women who are in today's workplace—women who know what it takes today to get the job.

ORDER FORM

TITLE	PAPER	CLOTH	QUANTITY
Cool Careers for Girls in Computers	$12.95	$19.95	_____
Cool Careers for Girls in Sports	$12.95	$19.95	_____
Cool Careers for Girls with Animals	$12.95	$19.95	_____
Cool Careers for Girls in Health	$12.95	$19.95	_____
Cool Careers for Girls in Engineering	$12.95	$19.95	_____
Cool Careers for Girls in Food	$12.95	$19.95	_____
Cool Careers for Girls in Construction	$12.95	$19.95	_____
Cool Careers for Girls in Performing Arts	$12.95	$19.95	_____
Cool Careers for Girls in Air and Space	$12.95	$19.95	_____
Cool Careers for Girls in Law	$12.95	$19.95	_____
Cool Careers for Girls as Environmentalists	$12.95	$19.95	_____
Cool Careers for Girls as Crime Solvers	$12.95	$19.95	_____
Cool Careers for Girls in Travel & Hospitality	$13.95	$21.95	_____
		SUBTOTAL	_____

VA Residents add 4½% sales tax   _____
Shipping/handling $5.00+ $5.00
$1.50 for each additional book order (__ x $1.50)   _____

                                        TOTAL ENCLOSED _____

SHIP TO: (street address only for UPS or RPS delivery)
Name: _____
Address: _____

❐ I enclose check/money order for $ _____ made payable to Impact Publications
❐ Charge $ _____ to: ❐ Visa ❐ MasterCard ❐ AmEx ❐ Discover

Card #: _____   Expiration: _____
Signature: _____   Phone number: _____

Phone toll-free at 1-800/361-1055, or fax/mail/email your order to:
IMPACT PUBLICATIONS 9104 Manassas Drive, Suite N, Manassas Park, VA 20111-5211
Fax: 703/335-9486; email: orders@impactpublications.com